Also by Adam-Troy Castro

Fiction

Lost in Booth Nine

X-Men/Spider-Man: Time's Arrow Book 2, The Present (with Tom
DeFalco)

Spider-Man: The Gathering of the Sinister Six

An Alien Darkness

A Desperate, Decaying Darkness

Spider-Man: The Revenge of the Sinister Six

Spider-Man: The Secret of the Sinister Six

The Sinister Six Combo

Vossoff and Nimmitz: Just a Couple of Idiots Reupholstering Space and
Time

Tangled Strings

With the Stars in Their Eyes (with Jerry Oltion)

The Shallow End of the Pool (Forthcoming, Creeping Hemlock Press, 2007)

Emissaries from the Dead (Forthcoming, HarperCollins, 2008)

Nonfiction

"My Ox is Broken!": Detours, Roadblocks, Fast Forwards, and Other Great
Moments from TV's The Amazing Race

THE
Unauthorized
Harry Potter

Everything You Ever Wanted to Know
about the Harry Potter Series

Adam~Troy Castro

Printed in the United States of America
10 9 8 7 6 5 4 3 2 1

Developed for Borders, Inc., by BenBella Books, Inc.
Send feedback to feedback@benbellabooks.com

Library of Congress Cataloging-in-Publication Data is available for this title.

Proofreading by Sean Sweeney & Jennifer Thomason
Cover illustration by Ralph Voltz
Cover design by Laura Watkins
Text design and composition by Laura Watkins
Printed by Victor Graphics, Inc.

To Devin, who devours each one at a single sitting.

Table of Contents

Prologue ... ix

The Canon ... xv

Chapter One
A Few Words on the Subject of Spoiling ... 1

Chapter Two
What's Not the Matter with Harry? ... 7

Chapter Three
Harry the Unknowing ... 17

Chapter Four
Hogwarts the Dangerous ... 23

Chapter Five
Magic and Muggles ... 29

Chapter Six
Hagrid the Deliverer ... 39

Chapter Seven
Hagrid the Despised ... 47

Chapter Eight
Ron the Weasley ... 53

Chapter Nine
Ron the Sidekick ... 59

Chapter Ten
Hermione: Daughter of Dentists ... 65

Chapter Eleven
Hermione the Know-It-All ... 69

Chapter Twelve
Dumbledore the Mysterious ... 75

Chapter Thirteen
Dumbledore the Headmaster ... 83

Chapter Fourteen
Snape the Enigma ... 91

Chapter Fifteen
Snape Undercover ... 101

Chapter Sixteen
Voldemort the Pivot ... 111

Chapter Seventeen
Voldemort the Villain ... 119

Chapter Eighteen
Voldemort the Crime Boss ... 129

Chapter Nineteen
Dolores Umbridge: Fear Itself ... 139

Chapter Twenty
Hogwarts: The Curriculum ... 147

Chapter Twenty-One
Neville the Wild Card ... 157

Chapter Twenty-Two
Divers Others ... 161

Chapter Twenty-Three
The Most Satisfying Moments in the Harry Potter Series (So Far) ... 167

Chapter Twenty-Four
Three of the Stupidest Elements in the Harry Potter Novels ... 173

Chapter Twenty-Five
J. K. Rowling: The Verdict of Posterity ... 179

Chapter Twenty-Six
Unresolved Questions: A Checklist ... 185

About the Author ... 191

Prologue

Welcome to *The Unauthorized Harry Potter!* If you've come this far, you don't need me to tell you what this Harry Potter stuff is all about. You don't need me to tell you who Harry is, or who his favorite teachers are, or why his childhood is a little different than ours.

You probably know about the remarkable success story of J. K. Rowling, the impoverished single mom who wrote her first books in a coffee shop and went on to become the most successful writer of all time, with a personal fortune that exceeds the Queen's.

You even know who we mean when we say You Know Who.

(Ssshhhh!)

What you may not know is what Your Friendly Host is up to with this book.

This is what we call, in the biz, an "unauthorized" book.

That doesn't mean it's against the rules, only that nothing here is connected to Rowling, or her publishers, or the other, many thrashing tentacles of the growing Harry Potter empire. It's the work of a devoted reader, who, like just about all of you, knows only what he finds on the printed page and sees in the motion pictures. It contains, I promise, no inside information whatsoever.

At no point during his research for this volume did Your Friendly Host blacken his face, use a grappling hook to scale the stone walls of the Rowling fortress, evade the attack dogs, crawl through air vents, descend through a maze of crisscrossed laser beams, snatch the manuscript from its pedestal in the throne room, photograph each page with a miniature camera, then slip away via the sewer system with the secrets sought by millions.

He isn't being paid nearly enough for that.

(And if that were the job the publisher wanted, rest assured that Your Friendly Host is not the guy they would have hired, anyway. You would know if you saw a picture of him. He wouldn't have gotten past the first step. He'd still be hanging on to that rope, outside the fortress walls, turning various colors as he struggled to pull himself more than one foot off the ground. It would not have been pretty. Perhaps fun to watch, but not pretty at all.)

No. If you read these words before that final book is released, be assured that you will find no clues to that final volume here. You know exactly as much as Your Friendly Host does . . . and, depending on how many times you've read the books in preparation for the conclusion, quite possibly more.

If, by any chance, you come to this book after reading *Harry Potter and the Deathly Hallows*, then you know far more than Your Friendly Host. You already know a lot more than him about such important questions as whether Harry survives (probably), whether Voldemort is defeated (definitely), whether Dumbledore and Sirius are really dead (possibly not), whether Snape turns out to be a good guy after all (could go either way), whether Neville rises to the occasion (he better), whether Hagrid finds true love (possibly), and who, among the long list of characters, lives happily ever after, or, for that matter, at all.

Since this book contains more than its share of theories about what's about to happen, you may even find yourself playing a nice game, in the years to come, with the pages to follow . . . which is to say, putting a little red checkmark next to all the places where Your Host has turned out to be not just misguided, but just plain wrong. Let alone all the places where I missed what will, in retrospect, turn out to have been obvious all along:

Dear Mr. Castro,

You completely MISSED the surprise ending where Filch the Caretaker turned out to be secretly Harry's father in disguise! How dare you call yourself an expert?

Sincerely,
A Fan

One thing's for sure. You also don't need Your Friendly Host as a source of Harry Potter trivia. There is no reason for him to fill these pages with obscure information like the names of known wizards, or the available information about Hogwarts students who appear only once or twice before disappearing forevermore. The publishing gods have already produced six books filled to the brim with such information, and another one is coming out this year—which is to say, the Harry Potter novels. If you want lists, then by all means feel free to make your own, with our blessing. We may even get around to something of the kind. But that, too, is not the best possible use for this space.

What you'll find here is some musings about the series and its characters, with both good and bad things to say about Rowling's accomplishment, and maybe some food for thought about the way she tells her story.

Your Friendly Host hopes only that this is as much fun to read as it was to write.

A couple of other notes:

First, Your Friendly Host is well aware of the existence of a religion known as Wicca. He intends no disrespect to the adherents of this belief system, which has been all too often confused with Satan worship. He knows that they're not even close to the same thing. He also knows that neither belief system bears any resemblance to the magic described in J. K. Rowling's novels. He uses the word *witch* as it applies to her fictional creations and with no intent to slur anybody whose personal religious beliefs may bear some distant surface resemblance to that fiction. So please don't write him complaining about the discussion of whether Muggles know that witches exist. We're discussing Harry Potter, not comparative religion.

Second, your favorite way to access the Harry Potter novels may be through the books or it may be the movies, but Your Friendly Host cannot proceed without admitting that he's absolutely in love with the audio book adaptations by Jim Dale. Dale reads the books unabridged, providing different voices for each of Rowling's small army of characters. There's never any doubt about who's speaking and there's never a point when his performance fails to be, for lack of a better word, magical. Pop one of those volumes into your car stereo, on a long trip, and you may find yourself taking the long way home rather than arriving at your destination with the plot headed toward a cliffhanger. This means a lot for recordings that, in the cases of the longer books, last more than twenty hours and may require more than a week to complete. All of Dale's voices are beyond wonderful, but his vocal characterizations of Draco

Malfoy, Rubeus Hagrid, Professor McGonagall, Kreacher the house-elf, and Luna Lovegood are particularly fine. Your Friendly Host intends to devour the final volume in this form. He suggests that you try at least one of them, if you haven't already.

Finally, this book is written by a citizen of the United States of America.

He dearly hopes that it will be read and enjoyed by some people beyond his shores.

If you're one of them, hello there. Your Friendly Host hopes that we can enjoy some good times together, throughout the many pages to come.

But your presence does require a brief note, before we proceed.

That is, much of the English-speaking world knows the first Harry Potter novel as *Harry Potter and the Philosopher's Stone*. This was a fine and very appropriate title, perfect for the book under discussion, given that the Philosopher's Stone is a long-established mythical object in our own, real world. Mentioning it in the title was more than sufficient to establish just what kind of fiction was to be found between the covers.

For various reasons, including the common understanding (unfortunately based on fact), that people in the United States do not spend as much of their free time reading as those in some other countries, the publishing powers that be worried that young people here would not even know what a philosopher was.

So the name was changed.

Within the United States, the book hit shelves under the title *Harry Potter and the Sorcerer's Stone*. The text was changed, too, ensuring that the magical object in question was a sorcerer's stone and not a philosopher's stone, wherever it appeared.

This title change was preserved by the movie adaptation.

To our foreign friends: Please know that Your Friendly Host regrets this. He's on your side. He does believe *Philosopher's Stone* to be, by far, the better title.

However, he did first encounter the book under its American title *Sorcerer's Stone*. And he knows that his book will reach the vast majority of its readers within the United States, where most know only the altered title.

So he has to make a difficult tactical decision here.

He could spend the entirety of this book referring to the first Harry

Potter novel as *Sorcerer's Stone* (known everywhere people read books as *Philosopher's Stone*).

That would get old, right quick.

Or he could simply use *Sorcerer's Stone* and beg the kind indulgence of those of you who first encountered the book under its author's preferred title.

That's pretty much what happens here.

As long as you've actually already paid for your copy, those of you who read *Philosopher's Stone* and find the alteration jarring to your sensibilities may feel free to attack the following book with a fine-line marker and restore the title you venerate, in your own hand, wherever the offending phrase appears. You can even change it to *Moll Flanders* if you prefer. Or even *1500 Ways to Baste a Turkey*. This may be Your Friendly Host's living room, but you are his guests, and he wants you to be comfortable for the rest of the party. He hopes it won't be too bumpy a ride.

This last section of the introduction is called *The Acknowledgments*. It's basically the author mentioning a whole bunch of friends who helped him with the book or who were around doing friend stuff while he was writing it.

It's boring stuff, really, but authors get to do this kind of thing. You can skip it, secure in the knowledge that if you're not one of the people mentioned here, the following paragraphs are exactly as boring as you would expect them to be:

Thanks to my wife, the beautiful Judi Castro.

Thanks to Devin Mont, not only for showing us how enthusiastic Harry Potter fans can be, but for reigning in that enthusiasm when we assured him we honestly did not want him to tell us, ahead of time, whose death scene he had just read. We know that he found it difficult to keep quiet, and we thank him for not giving in to his baser temptations. See chapter one for more details.

Thanks to George Peterson, who cackles out loud whenever he finds a passage he especially likes. Thanks to Christy Santiago, who pumps her fist in the air at the very idea of the next volume coming out. Thanks to Chris Negelein, who will get a copy of the next Harry Potter book if he ever manages to find the street the bookstore's on. Thanks to Melanie Herz and Dina Pearlman for friendship. Thanks to Jill, Kevin, Zach, Kate, Ari, Chuckie, Lola, Schlomie, Casey, and Dakota. Thanks to Uma,

Maggie, Farrow, and Ralphie. Thanks to Glenn Yeffeth, who is no doubt bemused to find his own name listed immediately after three dogs, two horses, and four cats: a fine indication of exactly where editors stand, in the scheme of things. (Rest assured that were I to acknowledge myself, my own listing would come somewhere long after that.) Thanks to Jennifer Thomason. Thanks to Joshua Bilmes and Scott Edelman. Thanks to Joey and Debbie Green, to David Goodman, and to Janna Silverstein. Thanks to the members of the South Florida Science Fiction Society writer's workshop: the aforementioned George Peterson, Wade Brown, Dave Dunn, Ben Burgis, Cliff Dunbar, the aforementioned Christopher Negelein, Mitch Silverman, Brad Aiken, and Terri Wells. Thanks to the various denizens of my newsgroup on www.sff.net, who keep nudging me for details on every little bit of minutiae that escapes my head. (I'm *still* talking to you, Michael Burstein.) Thanks to Borders Books for the opportunity to vent.

Thanks to J. K. Rowling, for doing the one thing that all great writers of fiction need to do: which is to say, make us forget the weight of the book in our hands, and lose all track of time in our desperate hunger to discover what happens next.

And thanks to Harry, Hermione, Ron, and the rest of the Hogwarts gang: this one's for you, kids!

Adam-Troy Castro
December 12, 2006
Miami, Florida

The Canon

(Now Complete)

Harry Potter and the Sorcerer's Stone

Harry Potter and the Chamber of Secrets

Harry Potter and the Prisoner of Azkaban

Harry Potter and the Goblet of Fire

Harry Potter and the Order of the Phoenix

Harry Potter and the Half-Blood Prince

Harry Potter and the Deathly Hallows

A Few Words on the Subject of Spoiling

Before we get into matters involving Harry Potter proper, let us expend a paragraph or two involving proper behavior around carefully guarded plot points.

Your Friendly Host begins by warning that this book assumes that you've already read the first six Harry Potter novels, or failing that, do not care if he gives away their most critical surprises. He knows that without this understanding you'll be really upset at him if you blunder onto some later page and find out, for instance, that ****** ***** ** ********, let alone that ***** ***** *********. So he warns that, following this paragraph, he will not hide such sensitive information behind asterisks.

Again: if you proceed beyond this point, do so at your own risk. At least one major plot point, from a past book, will be spoiled within the next couple of pages. An even bigger one will be spoiled not long after that.

Further spoilers will occur several times a chapter.

Your Friendly Host does not want you getting there unless you've already been there, or honestly don't mind.

He goes there himself because *that's the kind of book this is.*

It will have that kind of thing in it, and he wants you fairly warned.

So stop here, unless you're ready for it.

That said, let's talk a little bit about spoilage in general.

One young man dear to us seized each of the last Harry Potter books during the midnight sales held at the massive book store near his home. Showing a deep enthusiasm and abiding love of the series, he camped out late at night, seized his copy the instant it was uncrated by store employees, stood in line with it clutched to his breast, went home, and then spent the rest of that long and sleepless night perusing every word so he could be finished by breakfast the next morning.

This is not uncommon behavior for Harry Potter fans.

The enthusiasm is what makes the epic's effect on readers so special.

But all the energy and all the love and all of his deep personal involvement with the material left this young man hopping up and down with the wonderfulness he had just experienced.

He ached to tell somebody.

This was especially vexing to him, because this particular Harry Potter novel was one of the several that came complete with advance word that somebody important to Harry Potter met a tragic end in its pages.

Fans had spent months debating whose character's head rested on the chopping block. Was it Ron? Was it Hermione? Was it Hagrid?

Now our young friend knew. And he ached to talk about what had just happened.

This only became a problem when he encountered those of us who enjoy the series just as much as he does but preferred to spend the night of the book's release in bed, with our eyes closed. It was a terrible frustration to him that his partners in enthusiasm had literally fallen asleep on the job when there was a story to talk about, a secret to share. Burning with the need to tell, he asked whether we minded having the secret ruined.

We said we did mind.

This stopped him in mid-gush.

He had not expected this answer.

He had expected us to say, "Sure, go ahead."

Still jumping up and down with excess energy, he offered a deal. He would present us with a list of characters that included the dear departed among a number who still remained alive and well. That way we would at least have a clue.

He said, "Okay. It's one of these these three people—"

But this remained more than we wanted to know.

We said, "No. Please don't."

He said, "Pleaaaaaaaaseeee . . ."

We had to insist: "No."

The point was that we wanted to get to that character's death scene, however it happened, whenever we happened to reach it. We understood why this young man wanted to tell us, but needed him to resist with all due respect to our own preference.

We give him credit. He resisted the dearest desire of his heart and kept his mouth shut, enabling us to enjoy the story for ourselves.

And that's why we were able to feel every ounce of young Harry's grief and despair, at the apparent death of Harry's stepfather, Sirius Black, in *Harry Potter and the Order of the Phoenix.*

(You were warned. I spent a full page warning you. If what I just said spoils things for you, stop reading now. Because another one is coming up.)

Now, let us compare this young man's self-restraint with the actions of another young man we know about. Say what you will about our friend: his urge to blurt out the secret came from a genuine love for the Harry Potter books, and a need to share something he treasured with people he treasured. He resisted the temptation out of sincere respect for what we wanted and needed.

This other fellow's interest in revealing major plot points was something else.

It was not based on love for the books, at all.

It was cynical and superior and just plain malicious.

Here's a guy who should have known better, who thought ruining the book for other people was downright hilarious.

So what he did was snag his own copy of the latest volume, *Harry Potter and the Half-Blood Prince,* at one of these first-day midnight sales, at a superstore in Dallas.

He searched the book until he found the dread secret, and then he retreated to the mini-van he had borrowed from his mother.

By now it was 1:02 A.M. People were still leaving the store, books in hand.

We know from the time of night that he had not read the entire book. Oh, it's possible that he was an incredibly fast reader, capable of digesting a 700-page book in the one hour since the books were released for sale, but from his moronic behavior it's pretty safe to say that we're not talking about that kind of savant.

Rather, we're talking about a guy whose only interest in the book was, in his own words, "ruining" the enjoyment of total strangers, a guy who was so proud about his ability to spoil something other people enjoyed that he actually arranged for a video camera to film him as he drove past the crowds of late-night book buyers, repeatedly shouting out the words, "Snape kills Dumbledore!"

He was so proud of the anguished cries he caused that he posted the footage of his prank online. If you care, you can find it at the following URL: http://www.youtube.com/watch?v=TpO86uRReT0.

We offer the URL only to establish that we're not making this up. Given the choice, we would prefer you to ignore it, and not give this young dunce the attention he craves. (After all, we've already "spoiled" his own big moment. The clip itself adds nothing.)

It's a fair punishment. Given this young fellow's idea of what's funny, and what's worth doing at 1:02 in the morning, chances are that this will be the closest he will ever come to ever meriting attention from anybody.

We tell these two stories only to note the difference between these two young men.

The first wanted to spoil out of love. The second wanted to spoil out of random cruelty. The first resisted. The second gave in.

We know which we prefer.

But we also know that there will still be an awful lot of spoilage going on, on the day that the final Harry Potter novel comes out.

It may be true that, once these books enter the realm of history, and such secrets as Harry's eventual fate become common knowledge to anybody who cares to ask (whether they actually go to the effort of reading the books or not), "spoiling" will turn out to be nothing of the kind.

There are any number of great books and great movies that remain close to our hearts after we're no longer able to visit them for the first time. We can always find out, without reading the books, how Tom Sawyer escapes from Injun Joe, the sad things that happen to the Joad family, and how Hercule Poirot unravels the Murder on the Orient Express. We continue to enjoy the books, even if we come to them with those endings revealed ahead of time, and with the joys to be found there no longer including the thrill of uncertainty. We suspect that the Harry Potter books will also enjoy that status long after they've been leeched of all surprises.

But it's still a cruddy thing to do.

And to the extent that these words can light a candle against that darkness, we can only ask: "Please? Don't?"

CHAPTER TWO

What's Not the Matter with Harry?

Thereʼs something strangely miraculous about Harry Potter. Weʼre not talking about his ability, even as an infant, to survive the spells of Lord Voldemort. Nor are we talking about his gift at Parseltongue, or his genius at Quidditch, or his bravery in the face of certain death.

These all go along with the business of being a hero.

The real question is why heʼs able to function at all.

This is a kid who, from a very young age, knew nothing but scorn and mistreatment, at the hands of his vile relatives, the Dursleys. He did not experience severe physical abuse, as far as we know, but he was demeaned, deprived of love, and constantly reminded that he was considered less than nothing.

He wasnʼt even permitted the solace of friendship outside the home. As Rowling reminds us more than once, Dudley took care of that, by bullying any other kid who considered befriending Harry.

In the real world, this might have caused Harry more permanent damage than it seems to.

Depending on the awfulness of the treatment and the inner strength of the child, the life Harry experienced under the control of the Dursleys could have affected him in any number of nasty ways.

He could have become an angry, violent kid, with a hair-trigger temper that manifested as violence at the slightest provocation.

He could have become a timid, withdrawn loner, so afraid of punishment that he rarely spoke, and even then with an apology on his lips.

He could have turned his rage on himself, in ways too terrible to dwell upon here.

He could have lost all ability to connect with other human beings, and become a lonely robot of a boy, unable to care about others or make them care about him.

Or he could have become a split personality, behaving by Dursley rules most of the time, and showing his anger only when he could release control of his body to that part of himself where he'd stored all the darkness he was not allowed to feel the rest of the time.

There are even worse possibilities.

Some children treated this way become monsters, dangerous to themselves and to other people. Some become killers. We will omit unfortunate real-life examples, as too unpleasant to discuss here, and instead focus on one from the books. As Tom Riddle in *Harry Potter and the Chamber of Secrets*, Voldemort points out that he and Harry have a lot in common. He makes a good point. A kid with Harry's potential, treated the way Harry's been treated, could have grown up to make Voldemort look just a little cranky. He could have grown up evil.

Dumbledore, who makes some awfully silly decisions for such a wise man, argues in the first chapter of *Sorcerer's Stone* that a childhood spent among these particular Muggles is a good way to avoid swelling Harry's head with the celebrity he has earned, throughout the wizarding world, by surviving an encounter with Voldemort.

This is, on the face of it, a little like throwing Suri Cruise in a dungeon for a few years, so she doesn't get too spoiled by having Tom Cruise and Katie Holmes for parents. Yeah, it would prevent her from having a swelled head. But so would proper parenting.

(No comment on whether Tom and Katie can provide it. I don't know those people. I'm just saying.)

In later books, it turns out that Dumbledore has other reasons—a good thing for our opinion of the man, since that first one makes him look a little dotty. But, still. Even considering the later explanation that life with the Dursleys is one of the factors that keeps Harry safe from Voldemort's minions . . . life with the Dursleys is a very strange definition of *safe*. It's the kind of safe that virtually guarantees that the kid will grow up miserable, and almost certainly damaged.

Which brings us to what may be the very nastiest Harry Potter theory ever proposed.

This particular theory is so very awful that Your Friendly Host won't share it with you without first declaring for the record that he doesn't believe it himself, not even for a moment.

He rejects this theory not only because the books themselves contain plenty of evidence against it, but also, frankly, because there isn't a single part of him that wants any of the following to be true. Believing it amounts to believing such silly ideas as there being no such thing as magic, life not being fair, or good not always triumphing over evil in the end.

And while we all know from waking up and living our daily lives that all of these silly ideas are sometimes true, the Harry Potter novels come from a place that works from a better set of rules.

Your Friendly Host reports this bothersome idea here only because it's his duty to examine every possibility, no matter how disturbing, or how comforting, to the forces of darkness.

And so he says:

What if poor Harry Potter is still trapped in that cupboard under the stairs?

Children treated as badly as the Dursleys treated young Harry Potter sometimes hold themselves together any way they can.

When there's no place to escape to, they invent one.

They build their own fantasy worlds, rich in magic and wonder, complete with imaginary friends and imaginary adventures and imaginary explanations for their problems.

Sometimes they're able to tell the difference between real life and make-believe. Sometimes they're not.

Sometimes the places they build for themselves have such complicated histories it would take many books as long as the longest Harry Potter adventures to keep track of them all.

Your Friendly Host knows of a number of compelling fantasy worlds made up by people whose early lives were intolerable in this one. I'm not talking about books, mind you, but delusions, created by people in pain.

These people may live and breathe in the same world where you and I do, but their eyes see only the places where they feel happy and secure and loved.

It's very sad, but it's true.

So let's imagine, for a moment, that you're young Harry Potter, living with a family that hates you, that never gives you any credit for being brave or smart or good, that never celebrates your birthday, that reminds you you're less than nothing to them at every opportunity, and that makes you sleep in the space under the stairs.

Let us assume that school provides no escape, as your bullying cousin makes it a point to also prevent you from having any friends.

And let's imagine that this is all you've ever known.

What would you do to make your life a little better?

I can just imagine you starting to daydream about the things you want most. And what do you want most? You want people to care about you and value you and see you as an important person. You want to be taken away to a place where people are excited to meet you, where you have friends and admirers and even family.

In this dream, the people who have mistreated you all your life are punished for it. They're made to feel small and ridiculous and sad.

Chances are, your dream will require you to come back and stay with them from time to time, for little reminders of how awful they are. (You have to put that in your dream, because if you don't, you'll prove the dream a lie every time you wake up and find your situation unchanged.) But in the dream, your returns to this terrible place you must call home are temporary. It's just a matter of time before magical forces grant you another escape that once again punishes the bad people for the way they abused you.

Every time you're "away," you're reminded that you never belonged in that terrible place. Your real parents were as close to perfect as your young mind can imagine. They never abandoned you. In fact, they died protecting you. And everybody you meet tells you how special they were, and how much you're like them.

You're told that the bad man who killed them died trying to hurt you.

You're also told that you're rich and that a lot of people consider you a hero, just like your parents were heroes.

How perfect is all that, if you're the boy under the stairs!

Especially if you find out, on top of everything else, that you also have an aptitude for sports, and get to enjoy the cheers of a stadium filled with your fellow students!

As the boy under the stairs, you would naturally dream all of these things, and take comfort in them, and consider them perfect, comforting explanations for why you sometimes find yourself living with the Dursleys instead.

But then, there's a terrible thing about dream explanations. The flavor of your real life rubs off on them.

So the awfulness starts to invade your dream.

The evil man who killed your real parents may be dead and unable to hurt you, but he keeps trying to come back, and you have to keep putting him down.

The magical place where you find refuge may be so filled with miracles that you consider it more real than the place where you've been trapped all your life, but the darkness you know at home keeps invading it, and finding ever more imaginative ways to hurt you.

Your fame, in this magical place, may make you the center of attention, but it also makes you a target.

You keep finding yourself blamed for things that aren't your fault, keep finding yourself mistreated by adults whose authority you're required to accept, and keep having to fight for your life, let alone for your right for happiness.

More and more, your dream world comes to echo your terrible real life. The happy endings and hero status you enjoyed the first few times you visited your magical place are replaced by narrower escapes, or outright losses. You may find out that you have a long-lost Godfather, but you fail at proving his innocence and must make do with occasional messages smuggled in secret. You may excel at a wizarding tournament, but you lose a good friend and endure pain and terror when the monster who killed your parents comes back, more dangerous than ever. You may return to your school yet again, but it's become a cruel place, where you must undergo torments like those devised by the unspeakable Dolores Umbridge. You may achieve heroism yet again, but at the loss of a man you loved like a father. And you may become the apprentice of a man you admire above all others, but then you lose him, too.

It's not so much that Hogwarts is no longer safe, but that Hogwarts is no longer an effective escape.

There's no doubt about it. The adventures of Harry Potter are exactly the dream that would be dreamed, by that poor boy under the stairs. They offer exactly the comfort that young man would want for himself. And they betray him, exactly as those dreams eventually would, as the pain they held at bay gradually seeped in to turn those dreams into nightmares.

If J. K. Rowling were a different kind of writer, and the Harry Potter books a different kind of fantasy, Book Seven would have to end with a final chapter much different than the one J. K. Rowling has probably planned,

This final chapter would end with the following scene:

> *Half an hour after the local police arrived at the house on Privet Drive, they led both adult Dursleys away in hand-cuffs, and remanded Dudley to Juvenile authorities. The Potter Boy was examined by a police psychiatrist, one Albus Dumbledore, who reported the horrific emotional damage the boy has sustained during a lifetime of neglect and abuse. He described Harry's ailments in terms that included attachment disorder, paranoia, and possibly even severe disassociative schizophrenia. For the Dursleys he recommended prison. For Harry he recommended a long stay in a mental hospital, in the hopes that the boy might be able to live on his own, someday. "Alas," Dumbledore con-cluded, "the chances of this young man ever enjoying an ordinary life are not good."*

It would not be a happy ending for anybody.

At this writing, we're still months away from finding out what J. K. Rowling really intends. But we know this much. We're safe from that ending, which would make perfect sense, in a different kind of story written by a different kind of writer.

And however the last Harry Potter book does end, in triumph or in tragedy, we won't turn that last page and say, "Yes, but for all we know, this could still be the dream of an abused boy, trapped with a family that doesn't want him and that insists on reminding him how hated he is at every possible opportunity."

It might be possible to think that.

If we tried really, really, really, really, really hard.

But we won't want to.

Any more than we're willing to believe that nonsense now.

We reported that theory because it's an interesting one, not because we believe it ourselves.

As we've said already, we don't believe it at all.

Because we have any number of reasons to believe otherwise.

For instance, even if Harry appears in almost every scene, the first book begins with one told from the perspective of Harry's future professors, as they deliver the orphaned child to the Dursleys. Another begins with one chapter written from the point of view of the Prime Minister of England, and another involving an ominous rendezvous at Professor Snape's. We can say that all three of these scenes, and others that do include Harry, are unlikely to be dreamed by a disturbed boy growing up in the home of a family that hates him. They're not his dreams. So the rest of his adventures are unlikely to be his dreams.

But that's the coldest and silliest of all possible reasons.

The best reason is that, as readers of the story, we get to decide how much we want to believe it.

Remember *The Wizard Of Oz*? It wasn't just the movie you've probably seen, but an entire series of novels by L. Frank Baum. (If you like the Harry Potter books, you really should try some of those, too. You can even choose to believe that there's more than enough room for both stories to take place in the same universe, with Glinda, the Wicked Witch, and their fellow magic users all graduates of Hogwarts, or some other Ozian school much like it.) But the movie ends with Dorothy lying in bed after the twister that began her adventures, surrounded by a family insisting that everything she's been through has been a dream, suffered after a nasty knock to the head.

If you read the books, you know that this is not true. Oz is a real place. She really went there. She really met friends like the Scarecrow, the Tin Woodsman, and the Cowardly Lion. She really defeated the Wicked Witch. She really met the Wizard. And when she visited Oz many more times, and eventually decided to move there permanently, she had many more adventures just as exciting and special.

But the thing is, we don't need to read the books to know that.

When Dorothy wakes up, in the movie, we know that what she experienced was not a dream. She may not be able to persuade her Aunt and Uncle and friends that she really went to a place with talking lions and scarecrows, but we know better. We were there to see it. We went on all those adventures with her. We cried for her and laughed with her and cheered whenever she did something clever or brave. It was as real to us as it was to her. And though, at the end, it looks a little bit like we may have been sharing that colorful dream with her, we're not fooled by those claims any more than she is. We know that it was a great story and that we're going to continue believing in it, even if there are some fuds among her relatives in Kansas who insist on saying otherwise.

The sequels just prove that we're right to decide this.

Thanks to J. K. Rowling, we've been with Harry as he tasted Bernie Bott's jelly beans, as he rode his first hippogriff, as he met Moaning Myrtle, and as he discussed matters of life and death with Nearly-Headless Nick. We've cheered as he played Quidditch and we've squirmed as he endured the interviewing style of Rita Skeeter. We know that, if you stretch the point, he might be dreaming everything that happens to him. But we also know that the same is true of ourselves, and the second you go down that road you're left not believing in anything. Besides, why think any of that if all it accomplishes is taking a little bit of the magic out of the world?

No. Thankfully, we still get to decide what we believe.

And with Harry's adventures as exciting as they are, we know what we want to believe.

We want to believe in Harry.

His adventures are real.

So that brings us back to our opening question.

Why wasn't Harry damaged by his time with the Dursleys?

At least part of the answer is that he was. He has more than his share of bitterness and anger. He broods. He can be baited. He doesn't just dislike the Dursleys, he actively hates them—so much so that by *Harry Potter and the Prisoner of Azkaban* it's become downright dangerous for them to bait him as cruelly as they did just a couple of years before. (Remember the plight of the thoroughly deserving Aunt Marge?) By the end of *Order of the Phoenix*, it's completely understandable that he would be angry enough to throw a full-scale, despairing tantrum in Dumbledore's chambers.

And yet. Even that isn't sufficient answer.

Look at him. He's not just a fundamentally decent kid, but an astoundingly decent kid. He makes friends easily, forgives people who wrong him when the apology is sincerely meant, and protects weaker kids even in the face of superior odds. And while he may sometimes be confused over

14

the right thing to do in any given situation, at least he knows that there is a right and there is a wrong, and is capable of picking right, which is more than you can say for many kids raised in families where the only lesson taught is to stay quiet and keep their heads down. He's even a hero, which is the most unlikely of all possible outcomes.

How could he have possibly turned out so well?

Well, here's a terrible and wonderful secret.

We all know Harrys.

We don't always know we do, but we do.

I'm thinking of a man I know who was treated even worse, as a child, than the Dursleys treated Harry. Not all the details were the same. Some were much worse. You don't want to know them. They're ugly. This man would have considered a stay with the Dursleys, being treated only as terribly as they treated Harry, a nice, relaxing vacation. At least he would have eaten regularly. Sometimes he didn't get to.

Suffice it to say that the people who raised him did not deserve him any more than the Dursleys deserved Harry. And that it doesn't matter who he was, because he's just one of many. It happens more often than you think.

Today, that man has a family of his own. He's kind and he's loving and if he thinks at all about the way he lived when he was young, it's only enough to remind himself how far he's come, and how lucky he is to have the life he has now. Somehow, despite treatment that hurt him and could have twisted him, treatment of the kind that has ruined others for life, he was able to grow up and prosper and become the kind of person he wanted to be.

How he managed to become the kind of person we would all be proud to know is as much a mystery as how Harry managed to leave the Dursley household the kind of person we would all be proud to know.

But if you want another reason to believe that Harry Potter's adventures are not a dream, think of one possible word for the trick he pulled off.

A word that happens to fit the world he escaped to, anyway.

Magic.

CHAPTER THREE

Harry the Unknowing

The next major question is: Why did J. K. Rowling make Harry such a newcomer to the world introduced in *Sorcerer's Stone?* Why is it necessary for the world of magic to come as such a major surprise to him? Couldn't he be a kid like Ron, raised by a "normal" wizarding family, who lives a "normal" wizarding childhood and enters Hogwarts already bearing some familiarity with the world poor Harry has to enter blind? Or, failing that, why couldn't he be a kid like Hermione, raised by Muggles, but studious enough to pick up the basics before he took his first step aboard the Hogwarts Express?

He could have been, you know. Without changing much of the plot, the Harry Potter books could have been written about any member of the cast of characters.

Imagine the books written from Ron's point of view. We get to meet a young wizard from a family of modest means, who discovers almost as soon as he boards the train that his best friend at school is a notorious kid destined to get him in all sorts of trouble. That best friend will be the target of all sorts of nastiness, some of which will rebound against Ron. Ron will have to keep getting himself in all sorts of trouble to help this best friend, who will always be richer, more famous, and more popular than himself. The injustice of it all makes Ron mad, more than once. But he remains loyal to his best friend, and though he never becomes the world's greatest young wizard, there are compensations. For instance, if Book Six is any indication, he's the one who winds up with the girl.

I would read that.

Or, you can imagine the books written from Hermione's point of view. Here's a girl raised by kind and loving Muggles, who finds out, to her astonishment, that she belongs to a powerful and ancient race of wizards. Because she's smart, she reads up on everything she needs to know, and arrives at Hogwarts more prepared, on an academic level, than any of the silly boys around her. But she's so focused on book-learning, and excelling at her new life, that she makes herself a pain in the neck, and for a while has trouble making friends. This is rendered even worse by her Muggle lineage, which leaves her the target of certain bigoted fellow students, who subscribe to a philosophy that target her kind for extinction. Ultimately, however, her better qualities make her the prized companion of the most famous kid in school, a kid whose troubled past has made him the target of Dark forces. Without Hermione's wise counsel, this kid would constantly run headfirst into every dangerous situation without the wisdom he needs to survive.

That would work, too. I'd read that.

It wouldn't take all that much extra tweaking to imagine a series of books written about the put-upon Neville Longbottom (the bad-luck kid who eventually finds himself in a position to fight the forces that drove his parents mad) or even Luna Lovegood (from her point of view, the only kid smart enough to see the conspiracies so bizarre that even wizards accustomed to strange events consider her a crackpot for bringing them up).

We don't even have to limit ourselves to the student body.

Leaving this particular set of circumstances, just imagine the stories you can tell about Mad-Eye Moody, the scarred and disfigured mess who got that way from a lifetime of battling evil forces. You kind of know he has some great yarns to spin.

Or, for that matter, Professor Dumbledore, the *One Wizard Voldemort Fears* . . . who, we know from the very first book, has fought and defeated Dark wizards before. Boy, what his adventures must have been like.

They all had adventures. They all have stories to tell.

No doubt they would even be good stories.

(Your Friendly Host has to admit, he really wants to read Moody's. Heck, he would even enjoy Gilderoy Lockhart's, even if they are all a bunch of rubbish. At least they'd be entertaining rubbish.)

Instead, we get Harry's story.

Please understand. We're really not complaining about that at all.

Our appreciation of Harry's story is, after all, the reason we have this book in the first place.

But the question remains.

With all these great wizards to write about, why does it make the most sense to focus on one with such a deprived childhood that he needs Quidditch and the Hogwarts Express explained to him?

And the answer, as it happens, is precisely that.

Because he needs it explained to him.

The wizarding world is a great and wonderful place. Its inhabitants feel the magic all the time. But, to a large extent, they're used to it; they see nothing strange about flying around on brooms, or traveling by flue powder. A large number of the miracles they deal with every day are so common, to their eyes, that they've become downright boring, and unworthy of their precious attention.

But certain wizards, like Arthur Weasley, find the Muggle world downright fascinating.

So let's imagine a book, sold in the Borders on Diagon Alley, about a heroic young wizard kid named Larry Kotter who discovers that he's really a Muggle. Let us further imagine that Larry has exciting adventures in Muggle-land, and that Arthur finds every page stuffed with exotic detail.

Hermione, who has lived in both worlds, would be unlikely to find much entertainment value in passages like the following:

The doors slid open, and Larry followed his strange guide into a tiny little room with railings along the walls. A control panel bearing a series of buttons, labeled one through twenty, hung at eye-level just inside. "This is an elevator," Larry's Muggle guide explained. "We use it to get from floor to floor in buildings where there are too many stairs to walk. What you do is, you press the button of the floor you want, and heavy cables hanging from pulleys at the top of the building lift or lower you as needed. It usually takes a minute or two to get where you're going. You just have to be careful not to get stuck between floors because it's terrible when that happens. I once spent an hour stuck between floors with nine other people that included a loud and angry writer. We all had T-shirts made up to commemorate the experience, but I'm in no rush to have that happen again."

(Please don't write letters. I know that the wizard world has elevators. I know that there's one in the Ministry of Magic. I just picked that phenomenon at random. I could have just as easily written a paragraph about telephones or subways instead.)

The point is that Larry, like Harry, is encountering something routine and commonplace in his new world, that few permanent residents need explained to them.

Anybody outside our world, who has never experienced such a thing, appreciates the explanation.

Anybody who has ever been on an elevator considers it a waste of time and wonders why we devote so much space to explaining it.

And were Larry the longtime resident of a high-rise apartment building, he would just ask his Muggle guide why he was being treated like he was stupid.

Similarly, were Harry Potter the child of a wizard upbringing who had already had all the most basic questions answered for him, nobody would feel any need to give him the simple explanations we need as readers. They would assume he already knew. This would be just as true if he was a kid like Hermione, an outsider herself who at the very least had the opportunity and foresight to read up on things.

Why did J. K. Rowling make Harry Potter such a know-nothing (if, in certain things, a fast learner)?

Because we the readers come from a world which knows nothing of the world he's just entered. We need it explained to us, too.

We're just lucky in that we don't need to make ourselves look stupid by asking questions.

We can ride along, invisibly, while he asks those questions for us.

CHAPTER FOUR

Hogwarts the Dangerous

Allwhich leads us to the nature of the place Harry finds himself asking all those pressing questions about the school he finds so much more fulfilling than his everyday life with the Dursleys.

And the best way to get there is to first talk about swimming pools.

I'm about to show my age, here.

When I was young most swimming pools had something called a Deep End. This was thirteen or fourteen feet of water, well over the heads of even the tallest kids, and expressly forbidden to those of us who did not know how to swim. Parents used to shout at us from the safety of their lounges, "Don't go in the Deep End!"

Many pools had a black line painted across their midpoints, marking the dangerous division between shallow water and that threatened, oh so dangerous, Deep End. A few even had a rope strung across the surface, at the exact same spot marked by that black line, establishing for even the most inattentive child the precise border of the land permitted them.

There was a certain thrill involved in paddling across that section of pool near the diving board, aware with every stroke that solid ground was so far beneath our feet that even if we could manage to touch it we would have to swim toward the light before we'd enjoy the chance to breathe again.

Now, you may wonder what Your Friendly Host is going on about. You may even have access to a pool with a Deep End, and find nothing at all unusual about these nostalgic memories.

But the fact remains that, once upon a time, just about every pool had a Deep End, and for a while now it's been harder and harder to find one. Stay at most hotels and you'll find pools a reasonably tall man can walk end to end without ever getting his hair wet. The same goes for many schools and public parks, and a great number of pools found in backyards. It's even become harder and harder to find pools equipped with diving boards, let alone high-diving platforms, unless you manage to track down one of the few pools built for that specific purpose.

This is especially true of schools.

And much of the reason has to do with the importance of keeping children safe.

We have become so concerned with keeping kids from drowning, from eliminating all danger in their play, that we have removed the risk rather than teach kids how to deal with it.

Now, I'm not the first person to complain about this. Nor will I be the last.

But that's where things stand in Muggle schools.

And it does lead us to the thorny question of what Harry encounters at Hogwarts.

During his first year, he finds one school corridor patrolled by a giant, vicious, three-headed dog. He ends up fighting a cave troll in a bathroom, and later fighting for his life against a teacher possessed by the most evil wizard that ever lived.

His second year finds the school terrorized by a supernatural creature capable of turning the unwary to stone. He tracks down this monster by finding a secret passage in a bathroom haunted by a student murdered during a previous school year. The battle that results almost kills him.

His third year finds the school invaded by an escaped convict believed responsible for murdering thirteen people, and guarded by creatures capable of sucking the souls from their victims.

His fourth year finds the school hosting a competition where under-age kids are encouraged to battle vicious dragons, risk drowning, and be lost in soul-destroying hedge mazes.

His fifth year finds the school under the control of a vicious bureaucrat who enjoys torturing the students she sentences to detention.

His sixth year finds the school under attack again, this time by a whole group of escaped convicts.

The school's landscaping includes a malignant tree with branches capable of hammering anything that comes into range.

The school is surrounded by a forest that is home to creatures both strange and dangerous, including a colony of giant carnivorous spiders.

The school groundskeeper has a hard time distinguishing what is dangerous from what is cute, and is notorious for trying to raise dangerous creatures in his quarters.

The school's popular intramural sport is an incredibly dangerous life-threatening competition with a self-propelled game ball that, by *design*, tries to knock its players off vehicles traveling hundreds of feet in the air.

The school includes one required course, Defense Against the Dark Arts, that not only forces its students to confront monsters of every kind, but is taught by, in the first six years of Harry's attendance there, professors who are (a) possessed by mass-murderers, (b) frauds incapable of controlling the creatures they release in class, (c) ravenous werewolves, (d) imposters eager to conspire in mass-murder, (e) torturers, or (f) past followers of a notorious terrorist leader . . . the very *best* among them being the werewolf, an otherwise nice guy who is only a major threat to life and limb during the nights of the full moon.

Think of all that and think of Sirius Black in the fireplace, solemnly sharing a secret with his godson. "'Hogwarts,'" he says, in the tone of a wise man imparting a great secret, "'is no longer safe.'"

Thanks a heap, Sirius.

We might have missed that, if not for your keen powers of observation.

But, seriously.

No longer safe compared to *what*?

Juggling plates on a high wire over a pit of rotating knives?

Granted that many of the dangers listed above can be written off to the plotting of Voldemort and his followers the Death Eaters, many others (like those carnivorous spiders, and the insane risks that go along with Quidditch), Hogwarts was never the slightest bit safe. Hogwarts is a collection of bottomless pits vaguely organized into the shape of a school, and why wizard parents persist in sending their kids there, let alone why more kids don't end up dead, remains a mystery.

We can explain some of this.

The wizarding world, for all of its fun and wonder, is a dangerous place, with dangers that are not always limited to tumbles off flying brooms. It therefore follows that Hogwarts would include among its most pressing priorities preparing its students for these pitfalls. It can't accomplish this by limiting its lessons to mere theory (even if the hateful Dolores Umbridge pretends otherwise). It therefore has to expose the student body to the very same risks that they will experience as adults, and show them, by practice and by example, how best to escape these dangers with their souls and their skins intact. So that much makes sense, as long as the students are properly supervised.

The Muggle equivalent would be allowing grade-schoolers in urban areas to cross busy streets to and from classes, with the understanding that they won't survive long, as adults, if they don't learn about crosswalks and traffic signals.

But still, some of the things Harry and his fellow students experience on a regular basis remain a stretch.

Imagine how Hogwarts would change if its Administration was handed over to safety-conscious Muggles.

No first-year student would be able to ride a broom except on a carefully prescribed course, a limited height over a heavily padded field.

Hagrid would not be able to allow his students to hop aboard a Hippogriff unless there was a saddle with seatbelts that prevented the kids from tumbling over the side during an exuberant loop-de-loop.

The forest would be bulldozed.

The dangerous sections of the building would be sealed off.

Every single exotic animal brought into Defense Against the Dark Ars would be defanged, declawed, tranquilized if necessary, and only displayed to the students wearing muzzles.

The Monster Book of Monsters would be abridged . . . that is, published in an edition without a snarling, snapping face.

The Triwizard Tournament would be outlawed entirely.

Quidditch itself would be deemed not only inappropriate for students to play, but chances are also to watch, the theory being that no student should ever be tempted to imitate such a risky activity.

All teachers with questionable backgrounds would be fired as unfit to deal with children.

And so on.

It almost seems to make sense.

The thing is, we get a taste of Hogwarts under these kinds of restrictions in the form of some of Dolores Umbridge's edicts in *Order of the Phoenix*.

But that book also establishes why they would not work for Hogwarts. And that reason is, they have the unfortunate added effect of removing everything useful from the Hogwarts curriculum.

A Hogwarts where students are not permitted to deal with dangerous magic is a Hogwarts whose students graduate without ever learning how to deal with dangerous magic. It's a useless Hogwarts, and one that is even more dangerous to students who must face a world where curses and evil wizards and dangerous spirits are not just products of a fantasist's imagination, but very real problems that they might have to deal with at any time.

Hogwarts *needs* to be a dangerous place, for the same reason that swimming pools *should* have deep ends.

The Deep End gives you a reason to learn how to swim.

And if you never learn how to swim, that's when you're most in danger of drowning.

CHAPTER FIVE

Magic and Muggles

The greatest unresolved conflict in the Harry Potter novels is not the grudge match between Harry and his nemesis, Lord Voldemort. It's the one between the world inhabited by wizards and the one inhabited by Muggles, worlds that brush up against one another in any number of odd ways but seem to exist in different realms, which have little of consequence to say to one another.

It's an odd state of affairs.

And not just because it's odd indeed for trains to depart from fractional railroad platforms, mirrors to reflect anything but the sights before them, and pet rats to be anything but actual rodents concerned with nothing but where their next bite of kibble is coming from.

It's odd because this does not seem to be the way things would actually turn out, were any of this taking place in the real world with real people.

Your Friendly Host will explain exactly what he means by that, in a minute, but in the meantime, here's a secret of the fantasy trade. Any author of any fantasy or science fiction novel, creating an entire world from the bottom up, needs to juggle just how much gets explained because it's necessary, just how much gets glossed over because it's not, and just how much the reader needs to be distracted from because it doesn't really work.

Any reader of the Harry Potter novels knows just how much J. K. Rowling explains. She explains so much, through such happy-to-explain characters as Dumbledore, Hermione, Hagrid, Lupin, and so on, that for some readers the books feel like nothing but a collection of entertaining explanations.

Look a level below that and you will find all the things Rowling glosses over. Chief among them is the question of just how magic works. For instance, what powers it? Are witches and wizards living power batteries, with varying degrees of internal voltage, who just happen to be capable of tapping into their own internal energies by waving wands while shouting out incantations? Or is there some great, external energy, all around us, that wizards with no inherent power of their own possess varying degrees of talent at manipulating?

Rowling never says. Nor does she ever even bring up the question, or allow any of her characters to bring up the question.

She certainly avoids the third possibility, that when wizards perform magic they're actually appealing to otherworldly presences, like angels or demons or entities who fit neither definition, who for reasons of their own love to oblige certain mortals by performing miracles on command. Giving this one a wide berth can only be seen as a wise decision given how much heat she's taken from silly insecure people inclined to believe that her books encourage Satan-worship in children.

In truth, she's right to gloss over this key point. It powers her universe and makes it possible, but has nothing whatsoever to do with anything her people actually do there. She can put it aside. In this way she can also ignore who assigns given magical phrases to their respective effects, and therefore not have to explain why "Expecto Patronum!" would be any more effective at summoning a Patronus than, let's say, "Gimme a Patronus, You Red Hot Mama!"

The Dementors all stopped in their tracks, cocking their hooded heads as if dumbfounded by the words of the lone boy before them. Did the Potter boy just actually say that?

Your Friendly Host should point out, here, that there's nothing at all wrong with this. It's hard to construct make-believe worlds. And if you had to explain every last little thing you'd have no room for anything else. By letting this point slide Rowling is just following in the footsteps of the entire generations of fantasy authors who plowed this particular field before her.

And the same can be said of the way she handles the level below that, the realm of questions that the readers need to be distracted from, lest too much close examination makes the whole mess fall apart.

And chief among that is the nature of the relationship between wizards and Muggles, as set up in the story's very structure.

That structure dictates that Harry will find out that a secret society made up of witches and wizards exists alongside the mundane or Muggle one where he's been raised. This society is much like our own, except that it runs on magic, instead of technology. It has its own government, its own educational institutions, its own customs, its own wildlife, its own history, and its own set of physical laws. The two worlds co-exist and interact so often that the wizarding world's ruling body has an entire set of guidelines dictating how best to hide the very existence of magic from the Muggles who live beside them as neighbors.

This much structure is necessary, because the very nature of the story requires that Harry find out about his own secret birthright, and to enter the wizarding world as an outsider astonished to discover, not only that the place exists, but that he's a legendary figure there.

The story as designed wouldn't work at all unless Rowling is able to persuade us to accept that much.

For the most part, we do.

We do even though the first thing we notice is that the wizarding world is no secret to those Muggles who have had some contact with it.

The Dursleys, for instance, are well aware that Petunia's sister Lily was a witch. They even know that Harry has magical powers. They happen to find such huggery-pokery shameful and embarrassing, because they're so small-minded that they look down on any lifestyle that conflicts with their own, but let's be fair: given the kind of people they are, they'd say the same thing about people who read the wrong books or listened to the wrong music or wore the wrong clothes or voted for the wrong political party.

The fact is that they know, from personal experience—often terrifying personal experience—that the wizarding world exists. It's not a secret to them. And the main reason they don't talk about it is, not that they don't believe in it, but that they hope nobody will notice their own connection to it.

Who else knows, among the Muggles? Well, anybody else who happens to have a witch or wizard in their immediate family. Hermione's parents, the Dentists, know, and they're wholly supportive of her Hogwarts career, even if we get the impression that they're somewhat baffled. They keep the secret as well, though that must lead to some uncomfortable moments when the neighbors ask about how well their daughter's doing in school. It'll get even worse when Hermione starts her career (if she gets to start a career), and the parents of her old school friends bring up the accomplishments of their son, the Podiatrist, and want to know just what dear old Hermione ended up doing. But no doubt that being the Muggle parents of a witch means learning how to stick to their cover story.

Who else? Well, according to *Half-Blood Prince*, there's also the Prime Minister, who (much to his dismay) receives occasional reports on the doings of the wizarding world, from his opposite number in the Ministry of Magic. We can assume that the same is true of the President of the United States, and other selected world leaders. To be sure, these briefings are peremptory and uninvited and seem divorced from any purpose. The Minister of Magic tells the Prime Minister of England that Voldemort is on the loose and the world is at war, but also that there's nothing he can do about it. It affects him, but it is outside his jurisdiction. Gee, thanks a lot.

One can only imagine how Winston Churchill must have greeted his first introduction to whoever served as Minister of Magic, in his time. Your Friendly Host is not entirely sure it was printable. Or maybe it was. Consider a later meeting:

> The Prime Minister exhaled a plume of cigar smoke. "I wouldn't normally ask this," he began, "but we've been having a few problems with a nasty bunch just across the pond, and I was wonder-

ing if there was anything you could do to, oh, let's say, turn them all into frogs, or something. . . ."

Either way, we need to wonder whether everybody in the Muggle world would always be so scrupulous about keeping the secret. Wouldn't there be even one Muggle Mum, anywhere, who'd call up the members of her sewing circle to boast, "Oi! Vera! Did you hear me girl Deirdre's been picked for Slytherin?" No doubt prompting her friends to ask, "Oh, yes? Slithering where?" Fans of the comedy troupe Monty Python can already imagine the dialogue going on from there, in the suitably high-pitched falsettos of Graham Chapman and Terry Jones. (Never mind who they are if they're before your time, but you really should check them out.)

And now, The Ministry of Silly Spells sketch.

The point is that it would be happening. Despite any temptation, within the Muggle world, to dismiss talkative parents or other would-be-witnesses as merely a bunch of delusional nutters, the story would get out.

One easy answer, which Your Friendly Host warns in advance will prove inadequate, is that the word has gotten out. Those of us who live in the Muggle world have heard of wizards, witches, werewolves, vampires, ghosts, and other magical creatures. In the past, we ran entire Inquisitions to persecute the magical among us, though we had no idea how to tell a real witch from a merely suspected one and as a result ended up burning many of our own kind at the stake. Since then, with the rise of science, we have relegated all of that into the realm of fantasy, and reject it as the stuff of fairy tales and legends, fit for sitcoms, horror movies, and Halloween decorations but not for anything else. This helps to explain why Harry knows exactly what Hagrid's talking about, when the giant tells him about his wizarding birthright. He's familiar with the concept. For all we know, he's even read The Lord of the Rings, though Rowling spares us this scene:

> *Harry caught his first glimpse of Dumbledore. His eyes bugged. "Wow!" he exclaimed. "It's Gandalf!" He did not know that this innocent remark would forever shame him in the eyes of his classmates.*

We also know that there are entire Departments at the Ministry of Magic dedicated to keeping Muggles in the dark. They flit about performing cover-up duty, ensuring that any magic performed in public is corrected, and reduced to fleeting phenomena that can either be explained away, or ignored. The full weight of the law comes down on any witches or wizards who perform magic where Muggles can see it. Harry himself comes close to being expelled, more than once, because circumstances force him to break this rule.

All of that goes a long way toward explaining how the secret is kept.

What it doesn't explain—and what J. K. Rowling labors to distract us from—is the question, "Why?"

Just who is this law intended to protect?

We know it can't be intended to protect wizards from Muggles. Their numbers seem to be much smaller, but we know from a report Harry completes for school that any Muggle attempting to burn witches, in the past, was doomed to failure. We can assume the same of any other weapons the Muggles might bring to the fight. The wizarding world is vulnerable to daggers and poisons and even (as both Harry and Draco find out, to their sorrow) solid punches to the face. From this we can only infer serious vulnerability to bullets and chemical weapons and bombs and all the other wonderful toys those of us who belong to the non-magical persuasion enjoy turning on one another. If it came to a full, all-out war, a wizarding population capable of Apparition and Transformation in self-defense, and a wide variety of spells that include the Unforgivable Curses in aggressive offense, has little to worry about when it comes to any concerted attack by enraged Muggles. There would be bloodshed on both sides, but once alerted the wizards would be a lot better at protecting themselves, if only by Apparating away . . . and the battle would still be over the second somebody used the Polyjuice Potion to take the place of whoever's calling the shots on the Muggle side of the battlefield.

So that's not it.

Could it be that these protective measures are designed to protect Muggles from wizards? The equivalent of an endangered-species act, a goodwill measure enacted by wizards for wizards to keep them from abusing their power over the less fortunate?

Unfortunately, that doesn't make much sense either.

And that's where we return to Your Friendly Host's statement, a few pages ago, that none of this resembles the way things would actually turn out, were any of this taking place on a real planet.

Because the wizarding world has never been all about the feelings and the rights of the less fortunate.

We know this because of Draco Malfoy sneering "'Mudblood!'" at Hermione.

Because of Dobby the Elf, living as Lucius Malfoy's abused slave.

Because of the Giants, who have been driven from their prior habitat and now live in dwindling numbers, under less-than-ideal circumstances.

Because of the centaurs, resentful from past slights.

Because of Dolores Umbridge, who, because she perceives Harry as a threat to her beloved Ministry, seizes every opportunity to abuse and persecute him, employing techniques that include libel, torture, and Dementors.

Because of the sheer size of the following enjoyed by Lord Voldemort.

Because even Hogwarts itself, which as personified by Dumbledore is the wizarding world at its very finest . . . is dependent on house-elf labor.

Make no mistake. There are good people, in the wizarding world. We're fortunate enough to meet many of them.

But all of this testifies to a people fully capable of oppressing the weak.

A society that fosters bigotry, of any kind, and that keeps slaves, of any kind, is not a society that will look at one vulnerable group of people, in its midst, and say, "Well, yes . . . we can do whatever we want, to these ones over here . . . they're fair game . . . but we need to protect these ones, over here."

Or to put it another way, let's look at one specific example.

Lucius Malfoy.

This guy loves having little Dobby around, to terrorize and abuse.

And it's not just because he's eeeeeevil. That manifests in his plotting on behalf of Lord Voldemort. No, he loves having Dobby around because he sees it as his birthright. He sees it as something he's owed.

Do all the people who feel the way he does also work for Voldemort?

No. Many would draw the line at attacking their fellow wizards.

But they would have absolutely no problem with importing a Muggle or two, to work in their kitchens, and shine their shoes, and say "Yes, Master," whenever asked to do something menial and unpleasant.

They wouldn't even have to worry about their Muggle slaves getting their hands on a knife, or throwing a lucky punch. There are ways to prevent them from revolting. There's a curse designed to make people do things they don't want to do. There's a love potion guaranteed to inspire their single-minded devotion. When all else fails, there are any number of magical punishments so terrible that they can break the spirit of even the most freedom-minded Muggle. A few judicious uses of the Cruciatis Curse, as punishment for crimes as petty as a resentful look, might leave even the strongest Muggle soul happy for the relative comfort to be found in a lifetime spent scrubbing floors on his knees.

You don't even have to think of the Malfoys pulling something like this.

They're so powerful they can put on airs even in their dealings with fellow wizards.

But think of who else would be motivated to treat captive Muggles this way.

Wizards who are sniveling weaklings, next to their fellow wizards.

Wizards like Peter Pettigrew.

Do you honestly think he'd be an understanding boss, if given the chance to demean some poor Muggle, drafted from his or her full partnership at a prestigious law firm, to serve as his personal housekeeper?

Really?

Your Friendly Host believes he would be a monster.

At least Malfoy would leave his slave alone, as long as the work got done.

But Pettigrew has a lot of aggression to work out.

Now imagine that the law of his people has no problem with this.

He'd go for it, like a shot.

This is all terrible to think about.

And, to be fair, it's not all that far from the kind of future Lord Voldemort envisions, when he's put in charge of everything. So it's always been a possibility.

The major question is just why it hasn't happened yet.

The Harry Potter books could have been about a young Muggle child, growing up as a house slave in a world where wizards have taken over and now rule like kings over the Muggles who have to do all the heavy lifting.

Imagine that boy, growing up in the Malfoy household, after Lucius buys him for his son to use as a personal servant or even a pet.

Imagine that boy's comfortable, pampered existence giving way to harder labor as young Draco heads off to Hogwarts without him, leading Lucius to sell the kid on the grounds that he's a toy his son has outgrown.

Imagine him finding out just how bad things are, for some of his fellow Muggles.

Imagine him escaping and discovering that the wizards had a weakness.

The rest of the series could have easily been about him leading his fellow Muggles to freedom.

That's another way the story could have gone, with just the slightest change in opening assumptions.

In any event, just why the wizarding world devotes so much effort to hiding its own existence, from people who pose no real threat, and who would be easy to defeat and oppress if it ever came to that, remains a mystery in story terms.

Rowling never addresses it. She just ignores it, hoping that everything else works so well that nobody thinks to ask that simple question.

Here's the real reason.

Harry Potter's world is supposed to be recognizable as our world.

And such a world is impossible if it exists alongside a secret world of wizards, as powerful and as corrupt as those in the novels.

Even if the stories specify no genuinely persuasive reason for protecting the Muggle world from such knowledge, the wizarding world needs to keep itself a secret because it's only the existence of that secret that makes the specific structure of these novels possible.

The wizards we have sympathy for need to be determined to keep that secret.

They need to labor hard to sustain the illusion that allows the story to work.

They have no earthly reason to sustain this illusion, and it's not consistent with what we know of them, but they have to do it anyway.

And for no other reason than because their world can't exist, as described, without that one colossal assumption making it possible.

J. K. Rowling had to prevent you from looking there, by making the rest of the story as compelling as possible.

Your Friendly Host thinks it's fair to say that she managed it. . . .

says "yer" for "you," "ter" for "to," "nothin'" for "nothing," and so on. It's a working-man's dialect, the speech of a man born to humble beginnings who, to the more highly educated figures around him, still wears that taint on his oversized clothes. Combine that with his blindness on certain matters involving appropriate house pets and you understand why people who see only surface appearance persist in thinking him low-class or stupid. He's certainly low-class by the Malfoy means of measuring such things. And he comes off as stupid, though he's of average or higher intelligence. Chances are, had he been able to complete his education, he would have still had some serious problems, establishing himself in a career post-graduation. You can just imagine those sneers down at the Ministry. Nope, you don't want Hagrid in your Department. You don't want to send him to any important meetings. Just imagine that voice, grating on the ears of all the influential types who can track their own direct lines of descent back to one of the great wizarding families. Imagine how much he'd bring down the tone. Just imagine him clashing with the furniture.

And (though we get the impression, from the sheer volume of the cheers he receives at Hogwarts banquets, that he has other friends, among the student body), doesn't it mean something to you that the three students who treat him with the most respect are those with the least emotional investment in the wizarding world's social ladder? We have Harry (who knows what it's like to live at the bottom of the pecking order), Hermione, daughter of Dentists, (who isn't impressed by wizard families with impressive bloodlines), and Ron (son of a low-income civil servant). Not a snob in the bunch. They all know Hagrid's heart, even if they think he's half-daft much of the time, even if his questionable advice sometimes leaves them fleeing from carnivorous spiders.

Dumbledore, an excellent judge of character in all matters not involving Snape (and the jury's still out on that one) respects him, too, in ways that include providing him with a home when he had nowhere else to go. It's no wonder Hagrid sets such store in him. But even Dumbledore can do only so much for him. He cannot change the minds of an entire society. He cannot force sense into the heads of the people who will despise Hagrid on sight.

In all these ways, Hagrid provides a fine introduction to the sad truth hidden behind the flashy surface of the wizarding world, the one Harry first encounters in the snobbery of Draco Malfoy, sees anew in the plight of Dobby the house-elf, and finds best illustrated in that self-serving sculpture of brotherhood between wizards, elves, and centaurs, at the Ministry of Magic.

Namely, that it's just as corrupt, just as bigoted, and just as unfair as our own.

Good people are hurt because of it.

The existence of an enemy like Voldemort who defines Ultimate Evil does not necessarily mean that your own side embodies an Ultimate Good.

Your own side can suck, too.

It is this that Harry learns at the hands of Dolores Umbridge, from the self-serving blatherings of Rufus Scrimgeour to the carefully sculpted lies that make his life miserable from the pages of *The Daily Prophet*.

He must learn all this so he can stand alone (or almost alone) at the climax.

It is the nature of a hero's journey.

But it all begins with what he sees from the injustices endured by Hagrid.

Hagrid has another important purpose, too, one defined by a powerful scene in *Half-Blood Prince*.

It is a moment that has been coming for several years, though neither Harry nor his friends anticipate it until it's almost upon them.

For years, they have endured Hagrid's Care of Magical Creatures class. They have hated it.

Oh, they found parts of it useful. Buckbeak the Hippogriff was interesting, in *Prisoner of Azkaban* (though it's worth noting that Harry doesn't enjoy his flight on Buckbeak's back nearly as much in the book, where he remains uneasy throughout his short flight, and concludes that he prefers brooms, as he does in the movie, where it's made to look like one of the most exuberant experiences of his young life). And the thestrals prove invaluable for the ill-advised flight to the Ministry of Magic, at the end of *Order of the Phoenix*. But by and large, Harry and friends find Hagrid's class dull and pointless. They endure it only because of their immense respect for the teacher.

Then the sixth year, *Half-Blood Prince*, arrives, and none of our three protagonists find that they can justify keeping Care of Magical Creatures on their respective course schedules.

They drop it.

What follows is a very real moment.

Hagrid, who is also upset because his good friend Aragog is dying, opens his front door to them, sees them standing at his threshold, and slams the door on them.

Harry gets him to answer the door again only by threatening to blast it down.

Hagrid, furious, yells at "Potter" for showing such disrespect for a teacher.

Harry stuns him by calling him sir.

Hagrid says, "Since when have yeh called me 'sir'?"

Harry responds, "Since when have you called me 'Potter'?" (*Half-Blood Prince* 228).

Take a close look at the self-loathing tone of Hagrid's response to that. He's hurt, alienated, and heartbroken at the seeming betrayal of three kids who have always been his friends. His feelings have been terribly wounded. But if you read his words, he's also attacking himself for being outsmarted, for being lonely, for ever daring to think that these three kids actually respected him.

He's wrong, of course. They respect him a lot.

They're not visiting him out of pity, but out of genuine concern for salvaging their friendship with him.

The thing is, they were right to drop his class. It didn't fit anywhere in their respective career paths. Continuing with it would have caused them to fall short somewhere else.

But if you think Hagrid's anger and hurt here amount to nothing but childish petulance, you're wrong.

They've been building for a lifetime.

For this moment, at least, Hagrid is unmasked in their presence. He is again the big, lonely half-Giant kid who thinks he never really amounted to anything and believes he never will, the one who suspects even his closest friends in the wizarding world of secretly looking down on him. The terminal illness of Aragog, who Hagrid projects to be another misunderstood monster, likely to go unmourned, makes matters worse, but make no mistake: it's his own life that Hagrid grieves about, in this moment. In this moment, in the presence of three of his best friends, he has never felt so alone.

J. K. Rowling is so deft when it comes to matters of character (except, of course, with people like Snape who are supposed to keep us guessing), that she renders all of this crystal clear without ever insulting us with a full explanation.

It's a critical moment in our understanding of Hagrid.

But that's not all.

Because it's also a critical moment in this story about growing up.

Harry, Ron, and Hermione needed to drop Hagrid's class.

They needed to do it even though it meant hurting Hagrid.

They needed to do it even though they *knew* it meant hurting Hagrid.

But they had to do it.

Because that's one of the things about growing up that seriously stinks.

Sometimes, growing up means having to make decisions that'll hurt your friends.

Sometimes it means taking a different path. Sometimes it means walking away.

If your friends are true friends, they will understand and forgive you. Even when they've been hurt.

That moment in *Half-Blood Prince* is a key element of Harry Potter's journey. It is one of the moments that marks him as poised on the edge of adulthood, needing to make his own decisions for his own reasons. Another comes at the end of the novel, when he announces his attention to walk away from Hogwarts and go after Voldemort. A third will come at the beginning of the final novel, when he says whatever he has to say, upon saying his final farewells to the Dursleys.

They are all rough passages to make.

But that moment with Hagrid had to sting.

Ron the Weasley

Now we move on to Harry's first real friend his own age: not just in the books, but in the entire world.

At first glance, Ron is a thoroughly average boy: he's not a great student, he's no prodigy at academia or athletics, he's prone to more severe embarrassments than just about any other student other than Neville Longbottom, and just about everything he owns is a hand-me-down from the several older brothers who attended Hogwarts before him.

We later know him to be one of the best friends Harry could possibly have.

But our first important question is why he's named Weasley.

And it's not fair to say that it's because his parents are named Weasley. After all, his parents are named Weasley because J. K. Rowling named them Weasley.

And it seems a strange choice of name, given that no member of the Weasley family (with the possible exception of Percy), is weasely at all.

It's especially odd because one of the many things that J. K. Rowling does exceptionally well is make up names for the people that populate her books. Indeed, Your Friendly Host has long been of the opinion that she's better at it than just about any popular author since Charles Dickens, the guy who could come up with monickers like Ebenezer Scrooge, Bob Cratchit, and Nicholas Nickleby that are all so good at evoking the people he's talking about, that you're well on the way to understanding them even before he gets around to showing you what they're like.

This is a terribly unreliable way to judge people in real life, where you'll run across people with last names like Chubb who aren't fat and people with last names like Saint who are just plain awful.

But authors get to pick the names they consider appropriate.

Think of some of the other names Rowling has come up with.

For instance, let's examine Cornelius Fudge. The first name, Cornelius, sounds awfully formal. It seems to denote importance, wisdom, and authority. Fudge does not. It sounds almost clownlike. It takes all the air out of that first name, Cornelius. The impression you come up with, when you hear first and last name together, is that of important person, perhaps even a self-important person, who really isn't as on top of things as he likes to think. And isn't that a fine definition of Cornelius Fudge?

Then there's Severus Snape. Severus sounds like "severe," which we know him to be; also like "sever," which is sharp and threatening. Snape sounds like "snake," which makes him sound cruel, evil, and untrustworthy. You can't even say the name Snape without wanting to put a little sneer and hiss into it. Put those names together and we get the perfect name for the kind of character he is: a severe, threatening, despicable figure who arouses our suspicions (and Harry's) almost as soon as he appears. It hardly matters that many of Snape's actions, in the course of the first five books, are explained away in terms that make him look like a reluctant ally . . . or that even the murderous betrayal we get to see from him in *Half-Blood Prince* is presented in a way that makes careful readers suspect a reversal of some kind, by the seventh volume conclusion. The name itself makes him sound like a bad guy. Nobody's going to ask Snape for a hug.

We could go on.

There's Tom Riddle. Tom seems to be a friendly name, but Riddle adds a question mark—a perfect combination, given that Harry trusts Tom at first but later learns he should have questioned him more carefully.

There's Dolores Umbridge. That first name implies a kind of formal, old-lady sweetness, and the second is a homonym for "umbrage," which means a kind of self-righteous, morally superior offense at something. That is exactly the weapon that the character turns against Harry.

There's Gilderoy Lockhart. Gilderoy is close to "gilded," which means covering something with a thin layer of gold to make it look more valuable than it really is, and Lockhart sounds a little like somebody who expects you to fall in love with him. What a perfect combination of names for that character.

Luna Lovegood is a silly, kind of dreamy name, specifically related to "loony," that warns us to expect the kind of harmless, endearing crackpottery we hear from her.

Malfoy includes "Mal," a key element of malicious, malefactor, maladjusted, and any number of other words that mean Just Plain Bad.

Sirius Black is not only wrongly suspected of being a *seriously black-hearted* villain, but (even after that turns out to be unfounded) persists in his habit of turning into a big black dog. Sirius is, of course, the Dog star. Sirius Black.

Mad-Eye Moody is not, in either his fraudulent or actual incarnations, the sanest or most cheerful guy you would ever expect to meet.

Professor Remus Lupin's furrier tendencies are little surprise to any reader who happens to know that Remus was one of two mythical children suckled by wolves, and that *lupine* means "like a wolf."

All of which brings us back to Ron Weasley.

Who is anything but weasely.

Were he weasely, which is to say, "like a weasel," he would be dishonest, untrustworthy, and generally unsavory: all qualities that would seem to render the name more appropriate for somebody like Professor Snape, or Draco Malfoy.

On the contrary, he's exactly the kind of friend everybody should make on the first day of school. He's friendly, unpretentious, good company, and so down to earth that once he gets over his first excitement at meeting the famous Harry Potter, he (mostly) refrains from seizing any social advantage from this prestigious friendship. Further events prove that though he cannot hide the fear he feels when faced by something like Hagrid's spider friends (or his own mother's wrath), he is at heart a courageous boy who is always willing to risk his life for the lives of the people he cares about.

And yet, J. K. Rowling defames not only Ron, but also his large and for the most part quite lovely family, as weasel-like.

Why would she do this?

First, it gives Ron something to be sensitive about. He doesn't like comments about weasels.

But the real issue, with that particular name, is not so much what Ron and family look like to us, as what they look like to people like the Malfoys.

Draco, who sneers many of his lines, and his father Lucius, who could teach a special course in sneering were Hogwarts to offer it as part of the curriculum, make it clear that they consider the Weasleys low-class. They see Arthur as a low-level bureaucrat who never amounted to anything and the Weasley clan in general as a bunch of no-account disgraces who can't even clothe their children properly without requiring the younger kids to make do with inferior goods and hand-me-downs.

The Malfoys cannot be alone in this. No doubt they're just the only folks rude enough to say it out loud. There must be any number of snobs in the Malfoy social circle who seize upon the Weasleys as a perfect opportunity to feel superior to somebody. You can almost see them regarding the antiquated, dusty old dress robe that Ron must wear to the ball, and sniffing, "Well, what else would you expect from that family? They're *Weasleys*."

The readers of the Harry Potter books happen to know better. They've seen inside the Weasley household and they know that it's a fine place, where nobody goes hungry and everybody gets the love and support they need. They know it's probably a far better place to grow up than the Malfoy mansion, no matter how many cowering, abused house-elves they get to use as personal servants.

Ron, bless him, knows better, too.

He knows he's a lucky kid, even if he often winces at his hand-me-down lifestyle.

But "Weasley" is still what he has to overcome in life.

It's no accident that he hates jokes based on his name.

And it is precisely this that marks the importance of the scene where Draco Malfoy barges into that compartment on the Hogwarts Express, to challenge Harry's choice of friends.

By that point Harry has already seen that Ron's on a strict budget. He has already seen that Ron has to do without some things. And he knows that Ron is not one of the "right people" Draco tells him he will need to cultivate as friends.

You could argue that this scene is as important to Harry's destiny at Hogwarts, and the kind of person he's going to grow up to be, as his later ordeal under the Sorting-Hat.

He's not just choosing the friendly kid over the creepy one.

That's an easy decision.

(On a storytelling level, it might have been a more powerful choice had Draco Malfoy not been the kind of kid Harry despised at first sight. Imagine how much more this moment would have said about Harry, if Malfoy had been a charming, likeable rich kid, whose nasty side was obvious only to those who'd been with him for a while. In such a case, Harry would have had to choose between the likeable rich kid and the likeable poor kid, and his sense of priorities would have been well demonstrated by his ability to decide, from much less evidence, that Ron was the more decent of the two. Instead, Malfoy [who has already proven himself a brat in Diagon Alley], enters that train compartment oozing enough malevolence to make Harry's skin crawl, and Harry's decision comes off as a fairly easy one. Your Friendly Host probably speaks for you when he says that he wouldn't have wanted to hang out with the guy either.)

But even if it was an easy choice, creepy vs. friendly was not the most important part of it.

Rather, that was Weasley (poor but decent, disreputable but honorable, defined by character), over Malfoy (rich but despicable, powerful but contemptible, defined by social position).

And it would not have resonated so well if Ron's last name had been, let's say, Smith.

CHAPTER TEN

Hermione: Daughter of Dentists

We've already shared a few of our thoughts about Hermione Granger, while we were flailing about on the subject of Ron. Pretty much everything we had to say about sidekicks in general, as applied to him, also applies to her.

But she deserves some attention, too.

And we will start with where she came from.

J. K. Rowling has said, in many interviews, that she has no intention of bringing Hermione's Muggle parents on-stage for any extended part in the action. You will never see them clucking over their daughter as she returns home for vacations with wild stories about accidentally giving herself the face of a cat, or battling Death Eaters at the Ministry of Magic. You will never see them putting their foot down and saying, "Sorry, Hermione! You're not going to be hunting any Dark Lords while under *this* roof!"

Hermione's parents don't even have any lines of dialogue. We catch a glimpse of them, early on. They're the pair of rather baffled dentists who make a brief appearance, going off with Arthur Weasley, and what they have to say, during that conversation, or for that matter any other conversations involving the life their strange daughter leads, or the strange world that they have found themselves dragged into, is likely to remain a mystery. Though it would be amusing to spend some time as a fly on the wall, watching their expressions as Hermione goes on and on about things such as her friend's pet rat being one of Voldemort's men in disguise. You're just not trained for this kind of thing, in Dentistry classes.

They seem a fine opportunity for low comedy, if nothing else.

Why don't they play a role in the action?

It's not because Hermione is ashamed of her parents. We know she's a kind, loving, dutiful daughter who writes them regularly, visits when she can, and doesn't flaunt her magical abilities in their faces. When she is made prefect in *Order of the Phoenix*, she's delighted for the opportunity to tell them about a personal triumph they can understand. If she shares the more frightening parts of her Hogwarts experiences with them, she does so with tact and with full appreciation of their capacity for worrying about her.

Also given what we already know about Hermione's attitude toward them, Your Friendly Host is 100 percent certain that they provide her with full acceptance, and that they provide her with as much guidance as they can, which may not be all that much given the great differences between the rules of the world they live in and the rules of the world where their daughter spends her daily life.

In the years to come (if Hermione has years to come—and having to say that about each of these beloved characters is rapidly getting on the nerves of Your Friendly Host), if she goes on to raise a family of her own, she will no doubt arrange many visits to further confuse the Dentists with an entire gaggle of levitating grandchildren who love to do things such as turning the cats into teacups.

No, that's not why we don't see more of them.

We don't see more of them because there's no good place for Rowling to insert them.

For instance, we could see them reacting, with astonishment and more than a little terror, to all the miracles that multiply around their strange daughter. But we already know from Hermione that they're nice

It is, of course, vital to keep his appearances to a minimum. Were he to appear every day, providing answers and dealing with problems as they come up, then the books become about him, and Harry is no longer a hero, no longer even a sidekick, but rather a prize for all the grown-ups to fight over.

An absent Dumbledore, a mysterious Dumbledore, a Dumbledore trusted by characters we trust, and a Dumbledore whose input is (at least at first) limited to providing wise explanations at the end of each adventure, is a Dumbledore capable of casting a shadow that can only be diminished by the actual man.

This cannot be stressed enough.

Dumbledore is not all-powerful or all-knowing. By his own admission, he makes mistakes, tragic mistakes, that cause pain and cost lives.

For instance, he eventually turns out to have had a noble ulterior motive for abandoning Harry to the vile Dursleys, but (given their character, and their not wholly unexpected poor treatment of the boy), that was a bad move that could have resulted in the creation of another powerful wizard as embittered and as dangerous as Voldemort himself. Certainly a wizard as wise as Dumbledore is reputed to be, could have come up with an alternative solution that would not have abandoned the orphaned Harry to such a miserable childhood.

Further on, in *Goblet of Fire*, everybody knows something's suspicious about Harry's selection as a Triwizard champion. Many characters are unkind enough to come out and say so, though a few (like Ron, at first) lay the blame at Harry's feet.

Dumbledore finds Harry's naming as fishy as everybody else. Great. At this point, in this particular book, Dumbledore's a wizard only if you need to be a wizard in order to see the obvious. But, as far as we know, he does not then devote any real effort to figuring out what's up, or anticipating the strategy of the forces arrayed against Harry.

Think of it. Imagine yourself Dumbledore. You're responsible for the safety of a boy whose destiny you know to be inextricably linked to the destiny of the most evil wizard who ever lived. And now you see that boy drafted, against the rules, against his will, and certainly against the enchantments you cast to render such a circumstance impossible, into a competition that you know he is completely unqualified to survive.

You suspect, but cannot prove, that this has to be another scheme against Harry.

And so you have no other choice but to allow the Tournament to proceed, with Harry as one of the Champions.

So all right. All headmasters need to deal with politics, once in a while. But if you were Dumbledore, would you leave it at that?

Of course you wouldn't.

A Dumbledore as wise as Dumbledore is reputed to be, a Dumbledore who is the *One Wizard Voldemort Fears*, would immediately take steps to ensure that nobody tampered with a competition already known to be deadly.

Were Dumbledore paying the minimal attention you would expect from a guy that smart, he would watch the first two tasks go off without a hitch, and likely realize that the third presented the unknown conspiracy's final opportunity for some serious sabotage.

In the happiest of all possible circumstances, this happens:

> *Peter Pettigrew, who had been lying in wait alongside his master, rushed forward the moment the Port Key was activated. He could hardly wait to earn Voldemort's gratitude by disarming and immobilizing Harry Potter, murdering any other Triwizard champion who may have happened along beside him, and performing the Resurrection Spell that would restore the Dark Lord to his prior level of health and power. He was so very eager that he failed to notice, until it was too late, that the figure standing in the darkness beside the crypt was not Harry Potter, not some other Triwizard champion, but Dumbledore, the* One Wizard Voldemort Feared. *He screamed as a simple spell from Dumbledore sent him flying and earned the eternal emnity of the Death Eaters by proving to be entirely helpless as Dumbledore took the shrunken, much-diminished form of Lord Voldemort into custody. "It was easy," Dumbledore said later. "Their plan was so stupid that even the First Years must have seen how fishy it was. All I had to do was perform my own surreptitious investigation of the playing field, spot that unauthorized Port Key in the hedge maze, beat the Champions there, activate it myself, defeat the pathetic Pettigrew, prevent him from using the ritual to restore Voldemort to full health, and bring the villain to justice. It was a good thing their plan was so transparent. Had*

CHAPTER THIRTEEN

Dumbledore the Headmaster

So, while we're on the subject, a lighter contemplation. What, exactly, does Dumbledore do with himself all day long?

We know some of it. We know that he's traveled around the world, pursuing leads to the whereabouts of Lord Voldemort and his followers. We know that he shuttles back and forth between the school and the Ministry of Magic, dealing with the political pressures of the job.

We also know, from the Famous Wizards cards that come inside every package of Chocolate Frogs, that he enjoys tenpins and chamber music.

But what about the rest of the time?

What about when he's actually in his office?

What about when he's actually supposed to be doing his job as headmaster?

We certainly know, at least from Harry's experience, that Dumbledore spends only a limited amount of time interacting with students. It's very rare for him to take an actual pupil himself. When he takes Harry under his wing, in *Half-Blood Prince*, it's understood that the Boy Who Lived has been given a major honor.

We also know that, as far as Admistrative duties are concerned, Hogwarts is a place that largely runs itself. It's not like there are ever any problems with the kitchen staff. They're house-elves, who love being slaves and happily cook all day without ever complaining about their medical insurance or working conditions. The same can likely be said about maintenance to the physical plant, and upkeep of the grounds. We don't know exactly how much is courtesy of the house-elves and how much is owed to a building with its own magical resources, let alone how often Dumbledore and his fellow teachers are required to cast spells in order to keep any ongoing enchantments current, but suffice it to say that somehow, shattered walls are always repaired, blood stains are always mopped up, and the shelves of the Common Room are always dusted.

He doesn't seem involved with student discipline. At Hogwarts, teachers set detentions and penalties at will (sometimes fairly, just as often not). Nobody ever marches a misbehaving kid into Dumbledore's office, and tells him to just sit there, trembling, while the *Greatest Wizard of the Modern World* figures out what to do with him. No kid ever sits, knees knocking, in Dumbledore's guest chair while Dumbledore rifles through spell books in search of an appropriate punishment. Given how powerful Dumbledore is supposed to be, subjecting a kid to that kind of treatment is a lot like aiming a cannon at a gnat, but, again, isn't that what you would expect a headmaster to do?

Nor does Dumbledore concern himself much with managing his teachers. Much is made, in *Prisoner of Azkaban*, of Draco Malfoy's complaint against Hagrid, following the unfortunate incident of Buckbeak the Hippogriff. That one goes straight to the Ministry of Magic. Dumbledore does involve himself in the appeals to save Buckbeak, but would that sort of thing account for much of Dumbledore's day? Your Friendly Host thinks not. And except for Draco, who prides himself in being able to run straight to his rich Dad, there don't seem to be many other student complaints to worry about.

As for the actual practical quality of a Hogwarts education . . .

Oh, please.

It's true that Hogwarts has a number of qualified teachers who know their subjects—McGonagall and even Snape among them—but that seems more about their own talent, than any controlling effort on Dumbledore's part.

When teachers fall down on the job, Dumbledore doesn't even seem to notice.

Take Gilderoy Lockhart, for instance.

The kids figure out, fairly early on, that the guy doesn't have the slightest idea what he's talking about. One would think that news of his incompetence would eventually find its way to Dumbledore's ears, and that Dumbledore would devote a little more effort to making sure that the students weren't shortchanged.

Never happens.

Or take Sybill Trelawney. The kids quickly see through her, too. True, we do eventually learn that she's a genuine Seer who does get some things right, and that Dumbledore keeps her around for that very reason—but except for those odd moments, it's an open secret that almost everything that comes out of her mouth is total nonsense, useless to that vast majority of students who don't share her erratic gift.

The rest of the time she's so useless that Hermione, of all people, *Hermione*, with all her talk of respecting the rules and listening to teachers, walks out on her.

Dumbledore may need her around, but does he need her around so badly that the kids have to sit through her drivel rather than learn something?

Or, for that matter, painful as this is to note, take Rubeus Hagrid. We love the big guy. How can you not, unless you're a snob like Draco Malfoy? But Hagrid's not legally a wizard. He's not supposed to be performing magic at all, even if he does cheat from time to time, and cast spells from a wand concealed in his umbrella. So that's his first problem. Right off, from a legal standpoint, Hagrid's the equivalent of a Driver's Ed teacher who has never earned his license.

But that's not all.

Let's assume that the Ministry of Magic did see fit to provide Hagrid with some special teaching credentials after his predecessor, Professor Kettleburn, retired from teaching Care of Magical Creatures to, as Dumbledore puts it, "'enjoy more time with his remaining limbs'" (*Prisoner of Azkaban* 93).

And let's further assume that, like them, we're willing to overlook Hagrid's historically shaky grasp on the differences between vicious and cute.

But the fact remains that he's not a terrific teacher.

The first compelling lesson he ever teaches is the proper way to approach a Hippogriff. That's the one that ends with Malfoy injured and poor Buckbeak marked for an early grave. Sure, the incident is not Hagrid's fault, but that's not the point. What is the point is what happens afterward. Hagrid is so traumatized by the injury to one of his students, and so paralyzed by fear of it ever happening again, that he spends the rest of the term teaching his students about flobberworms, creatures so uninteresting that they thrive best when left entirely alone.

Aside from thestrals, another fascinating lesson that goes wrong for more political reasons in *Order of the Phoenix*, he never shows his students a creature worth looking at again.

You may call this a spectacularly unfounded assumption on the part of Your Friendly Host. After all, we know that flobberworms have a purpose when it comes to the mixing of potions. It's certainly possible that flobberworms and blast-ended screwts are even far more important to the practice of magic than Muggles can possibly understand and that every great wizard who ever accomplishes great things manages them at least in part because of a secret supply of flobberworm larvae squirming around in their own slime in the pockets of his or her robe. But that's not what Rowling implies, and certainly not what Hagrid manages to impress upon his students . . . unless there's one major wowser of a reversal still coming in the final book, like the following.

> Voldemort cried, "Aaaaarrrrrggghhh! Flobberworms! My only weakness!" and dissolved into a puddle as everybody stared at a much-underestimated Hagrid.

In such a case many millions of book buyers, not to mention Hollywood movie executives, are going to feel awfully silly.

But really, caring for the species seems to be the Hogwarts equivalent of finger paints, which is to say, the activity you present to your students because you're not sure they can be trusted with sharp objects.

In short, Hagrid's effectiveness as a Care of Magical Creatures teacher is forever being compromised by politics . . . and we have yet another Hogwarts teacher who accomplishes nothing but wasting the time of his students.

Dumbledore doesn't seem to notice that, either.

He doesn't sit in on any classes. He doesn't make sure that his teachers know their material. He doesn't make sure they know how to teach.

CHAPTER FOURTEEN

Snape the Enigma

O f course, Dumbledore's oddest decision, the one that baffles Harry and several of the adults among the Order of the Phoenix, is his implicit trust in the most unpleasant member of the faculty.

When asked, he stresses that he trusts Snape "*implicitly.*"

He puts a special emphasis on this word.

Implicitly.

He says it with a force that allows no argument, not even from people who know of Snape's past as a Death Eater, or who (like Harry), have endured Snape's many casual cruelties. He cuts off any arguments to the contrary, often with a curtness that borders on annoyance.

Dumbledore has been wrong about an awful lot of things in his career, but the implication here is that, if Dumbledore is right about *anything in the world*, something that's fair to question given the sheer number of things he's been mistaken about, he's right about this. It would almost certainly have to be because of some special knowledge on his part, because nobody else in the Order of the Phoenix sees how he arrives at this conviction. Sirius and Moody and Lupin remain suspicious of the black-clad, sneering Potions teacher, and so does Harry, up to the very moment that Snape seems to prove those suspicions correct by seemingly killing Dumbledore before Harry's eyes.

The mourning members of the Order of the Phoenix make sad noises about Dumbledore's blind spot, when it comes to Snape.

As readers, we know that it doesn't have to be quite as simple as that.

If we've read *Half-Blood Prince* carefully, we see several indications of prior scheming between Dumbledore and Snape, including among them that moment when a distraught Snape cries about not being able to do "it" any more. (The definition of "it" remains a mystery.)

We also see that everything that happens before, during, and after the actual moment of the supposed murder possesses the slightest tinge of ambiguity.

For instance, Dumbledore says he has a secret way of hiding people. Snape himself seems to agonize over the act. And, once the deed seems done, and a vengeful Harry tries to kill Snape with the *Avada Kedavra* Curse, Snape prevents him, crying that he won't allow Harry to cast any Unforgivable Spells.

This declaration could be *either* the taunt of a villain, or the warning of a secret ally in no position to reveal himself.

You've got to give Rowling credit. She's given her most important cliffhanger, the moment that motivates Harry, Ron, and Hermione to pursue Voldemort on their own, so many loose ends that it could mean, essentially, anything . . . all without sabotaging its emotional impact.

The thing is, we don't know if Dumbledore really did have an unshakeable reason to trust Snape.

We don't know if this bond, however valid, went wrong because of the Unbreakable Vow Snape had sworn to at the time.

We don't even know whether, as a result, Dumbledore is really and truly dead.

(Rowling has said that he is. But we don't know that he'll remain that way. Remember, this is a guy with a pet phoenix. There's wiggle room.)

But still, a common rule of thumb for a certain kind of story, which this series falls into, is *they're not dead unless you see the body . . . and sometimes not even then.*

Remember Wesley of *The Princess Bride*, who is "mostly dead" all day, but gets better.

Or Gandalf from Lord of the Rings, who plunges into that bottomless pit in combat with the Balrog, but shows up later on, with a cleaner wardrobe.

Or Spock from *Star Trek*, who is fried to a fine crisp, but recovers in time for dinner.

Or Aunt May from the main comic-book version of *Spider-Man*, who has had two separate funerals, with each death later explained away as some villain's evil hoax.

Another good way to phrase this rule of thumb is *they're not dead if the writer gives you a loophole* and there are so many loopholes in this particular demise that Your Friendly Host wouldn't give so much as a farthing to any collection for an Albus Dumbledore Memorial Fund. Especially since, as already noted, the victim happens to own a pet phoenix.

All we are left with, really, is Dumbledore's fervent declaration of trust in Snape.

We need to dwell on that.

If Dumbledore's trust in Snape really is based on nothing but blind faith, and Snape's subsequent betrayal really did take him by surprise, then Dumbledore's not just fallible.

He's an out-and-out idiot.

He has staked his life, the lives of his allies, the life of the boy who represents the only true hope against Voldemort, the future of Hogwarts, the fate of the wizarding world, and ultimately the heartbeat of every Muggle on the planet . . . on nothing but empty promises from a man recruited from the enemy's ranks.

And as a result, he has gotten exactly the end he deserves.

But that's a big *if.*

Especially since we keep coming back to his certainty.

The *one* thing Dumbledore must be right about, if he's right about *anything.*

The *one* thing we must trust Dumbledore to be right about, if we trust him about *anything.*

Something's going on here, and it's not just what Draco Malfoy would call the gross incompetence of an overrated buffoon who's seen better days.

We'll know for sure when we see the final volume.

But in the meantime, just who is this sneering figure who so completely owns Dumbledore's trust?

This is what we know so far.

Severus Snape is a half-blood wizard who, in his own Hogwarts days, suffered the abuse of the small cabal of mischief-makers led by one James Potter. The young Snape was a bookish, withdrawn sort who secretly styled himself the Half-Blood Prince. But James and his cronies saw him (with, we're given to understand, some justification), as the class creep, the kid they could torment and bully at will, just for the sake of amusing themselves.

During the worst of these incidents, arranged by Sirius, Snape almost died, surviving only because James saw that the joke had gone too far and pulled Snape back to safety. Since then, Snape has always considered himself in Potter's debt, an obligation he continues to pay, up to the present day, by saving Harry's life whenever possible.

Enter Voldemort. Snape, no doubt embittered by his experiences and welcoming the chance to avenge himself upon the world that had been so cruel to him, joined the Death Eaters and became one of the Dark Lord's most trusted allies.

Then he reported Trelawney's prophecy to Voldemort, causing the deaths of the Potters.

Nevertheless, Dumbledore, the *One Wizard Voldemort Fears* and the *Greatest Wizard of the Modern World*, trusts him *implicitly*, declaring that Snape felt unbelievable guilt.

Your Friendly Host needs to apologize, here, for continuing to stress this past all endurance. But he needs to underline the significance of this turning point. That had to be one *doozy* of a significant moment.

And before we move on, to some of the other things we know about Snape, we'll take special notice of the chronology here.

First, he declares himself in James Potter's eternal debt.

Second, sometime after that, he joins Voldemort's Death Eaters.

Seems a bit odd.

There are a couple of possible explanations for this (three, if you count the unlikely one, already disproven by the intricate clockwork plotting of the previous volumes, that J. K. Rowling doesn't have the slightest clue what she's doing).

One is that Snape joined Voldemort because he was happy to belong to anything, and had no real idea of how serious, and bloody, things were going to get.

There's certainly historical precedent for this in the real world.

The twentieth century was filled with political movements that attracted millions of people who were seduced by thundering speeches and powerful slogans, and would not have approved of all the blood and destruction that followed.

Snape could have become a Death Eater because he liked being the one people were scared of for a change . . . only to recoil in horror when the killing started.

You can even suggest that the deaths of James and Lily Potter were what horrified him into changing sides.

But that doesn't make much sense, either, on the face of it. The killing was long underway by the time James and Lily Potter were targeted.

Indeed, that was the night the killing ended.

Imagine how you'd feel about a guy who saw nothing wrong in helping a mass murderer, until the day that mass murderer met his match and was forced to flee.

Imagine him declaring, "Yes, I know it's easy for me to say now . . . especially since I was the one providing him with the home addresses of everybody he killed . . . but honestly, when he killed those last couple of people, he lost me. That's when he went too far."

You'd say, "And does this change of heart have anything to do with the fact that his side lost, and you're facing a prison sentence?"

And he'd say, "Well, I know it looks that way . . . but honestly, I'd been having my doubts about him for some time before that. I was probably always going to change my mind sooner or later. But this particular set of killings? I mean, enough is enough."

You'd toss the guy into the deepest pit you could find.

Like Azkaban, for instance.

Unless there was some substantial interval between Snape's discovery that James and Lily had been targeted, and the actual defeat of Lord Voldemort, Snape's conversion amounts to nothing beyond a desperate attempt to stay out of Azkaban.

The only other possibility is that he changed sides much earlier.

But even that's not enough.

Let's assume Snape changed sides halfway through Voldemort's reign of terror, or a third of the way through, or even a tenth of the way through.

Or for that matter, only a week after it started.

Just how much killing would have already gone on by that point?

How much would he have had to turn a blind eye to, or even participate in himself, before this fabled moment when he said, *"No more!"*

Imagine your own mother and father among those who died at Voldemort's hands, before Mr. Slow Learner finally figured out the difference between right and wrong, and ask yourself: Would you really give Snape credit for changing sides? Or would you say that no good intentions were shining enough to wash all the blood off his hands? Let alone earn him (all together now), for the rest of his life, the *Implicit Trust of the Greatest Wizard of the Modern World*?

But instead, we learn in *Half-Blood Prince* that Snape remained a Death Eater until the very end, fingering the last two people Voldemort ever went after.

No, something's wrong here. That version of events doesn't work at all.

So let's reject it and try another.

What if Snape joined the Death Eaters *because* he considered himself in James Potter's eternal debt?

Now, this is interesting. In this version of events, Snape becomes one of Voldemort's followers early on, because he's eager to belong to something and responds to the acceptance Voldemort seems to offer him. But doubts set in early. Maybe he witnesses some of the crimes Voldemort commits during his rise to power, learns about the even greater atrocities still on the way, and knows that he must do what he can to stop them.

Dumbledore, who has long suspected Tom Riddle's potential for bloodshed, asks Snape to stay close to the man, pretending loyalty and cooperating in small things so he can pass critical intelligence to the opposition.

Snape's undercover status is so very secret that nobody, except for Dumbledore, knows what he's doing.

And it remains a secret between them even after the war ends with Voldemort's failed attempt to kill the Potter child, because Voldemort might still be out there, plotting a return to power. If the Dark Lord ever became a threat again, Snape would still be considered loyal, and would therefore still have some use as a spy.

Now, this has the benefit of making a little more sense.

And it certainly helps explain why Dumbledore, the *Greatest Wizard of the Modern World*, would feel so confident about his *implicit* trust in Snape's good intentions: because he's already depended on the man for years.

If this is what happened—if Snape has actually been working for Dumbledore for that long—then the various members of the Order of the Phoenix are going to owe the man one huge apology when the war is over.

They *at least* owe him a dinner.

But again, that doesn't quite work.

Because if he'd been working for Dumbledore, delivering secret information to Voldemort would be an awfully weird way of showing it.

So other explanations are still possible.

Let's look closer.

Let's enter the point where Harry enters Snape's life.

In *Sorcerer's Stone*, Harry sees Snape for the first time and realizes, with the unerring instinct of a boy who's been treated with hate his entire life, that the man loathes him. His perceptions prove correct when he attends Snape's Potions class, and is greeted by the man's total, withering contempt. Snape's past as a Voldemort minion, his open hatred of Harry, and his delight in harassing anybody who can be identified as one of Harry's friends, all so completely mark him as Harry's enemy that Hermione thinks he's the one trying to kill Harry by seizing magical control of his broom, during the Quidditch match.

This is a fair assumption, given the evidence at hand. But it's completely wrong. It's later revealed that the saboteur in question was actually Professor Quirrell. Far from trying to bring about Harry's death, Snape, manipulating his wand in the stands, was actually trying to help him.

Snape also looks awfully guilty during an overheard conversation with Quirrell, which is easily misinterpreted as Snape trying to bully Quirrell into giving up the location of the Sorcerer's Stone. But again, any assumption of his evildoing, here, is completely wrong. Far from trying to get to the Sorcerer's Stone himself, Snape is confronting Quirrell about Quirrell's own attempts to steal it.

At the book's end, Harry learns from Dumbledore that Snape feels obligated to protect Harry as part of a debt owed to Harry's father James.

In *Prisoner of Azkaban*, Snape brews the potion that allows Professor Lupin some control over his werewolf self. Despite his strong dislike of Lupin, he brews a working potion, rather than attempt any kind of dangerous treachery. The closest he comes to betraying Lupin is his stint as substitute teacher in Defense Against the Dark Arts, at which point he surprises the kids with a lesson on how to recognize and ward against werewolves, an act that is easy to read as a strike against Lupin but which is also easy to defend as basic information the kids might be able to use with Lupin in the school.

Later, intent on nailing Harry for one of the boy's many unauthorized journeys off school grounds, Snape tracks Harry, Ron, and Hermione to the Shrieking Shack, where he interrupts the confrontation that ends with Sirius Black's vindication and the unmasking of Ron's pet rat Scabbers as the true traitor, Peter Pettigrew.

His demeanor during the episode is downright frantic, colored by both anger and loathing. It's easy to read everything he does here as the latest step in his vendetta against Harry, especially since he also threatens Harry with expulsion. But think about it. Keeping an eye on Harry is, after all, his duty, and while he still seems to relish the idea of getting Harry thrown out of school, protecting Harry from Sirius Black (and Lupin, who seems inclined to listen to Black), nevertheless seems his top priority.

And let's talk a little bit about how much anger he shows during this scene. Who is he really mad at? Harry? Well, certainly. He hates the kid. Ron and Hermione? Yes, that fits, too. They earn no points from him for being Harry's friends. Lupin? Well, him, too. As a member of James Potter's old gang, he's never been on Snape's cuddle list.

Sirius?

Well, he certainly has reason to hate Sirius. Sirius was also part of the old gang, and the one whose practical joke once almost got Snape killed.

But is that the only reason Snape hates Sirius Black? Can it be that he also hates Sirius because, like everybody else in the wizarding world, he believes Sirius responsible for betraying the Potters to Voldemort?

Can it be that he takes that particular crime more personally than he lets on?

Or even that he considers it a betrayal?

But for that to be true, he—

Hmmm.

We'll insert a bookmark here, and move on.

At the end of *Goblet of Fire*, when Harry is threatened by Barty Crouch, who is still at that moment disguised as Mad-Eye Moody, three members of Hogwarts come to his rescue. It is Dumbledore who strikes Barty down. But McGonagall *and* Snape are right behind him, their wands at the ready. Once again Snape proves himself ready to rescue Harry. And once again he puts his private feelings aside, shaking hands with Sirius Black despite loathing left over from high school.

Order of the Phoenix presents Snape at his most complex yet. Tasked by Dumbledore to teach Harry Occlumency, he starts off doing exactly that, even if he peppers his lessons with vocal reminders of his contempt for Harry. He tries. But the lessons come to an abrupt end when Harry enters Snape's Pensieve, and thus discovers the indignities the young Snape suffered at James Potter's hands. Snape is so outraged and humiliated that he drives Harry from the room . . . and again, he seems delighted by the prospect of Harry's expulsion . . . but that doesn't stop him from later delivering Harry's urgent message to the Order of the Phoenix, an act that proves vital when Harry and friends find themselves battling Death Eaters at the Ministry of Magic.

All of this seems to establish that, even if he is Harry's enemy, in that he wants to make Harry miserable and get Harry expelled, he has never been Harry's *mortal* enemy. Far from it. He has, rather, always been willing to go to extraordinary lengths to protect Harry from harm.

It's only Snape's demeanor, which remains hateful throughout the series so far, that prevents Harry from ever considering himself in Snape's debt. Harry continues to see him as a villain and not as an ally, even when (all together now) the *Greatest Wizard of the Modern World* persists in stressing that he trusts the man.

We've already cast some doubt about the villainy of Snape's actions in *Half-Blood Prince*. We won't go into it again.

But yes, something is definitely up.

The *Greatest Wizard of the Modern World* is, like many stage magicians in our own world, hiding a card up his sleeve, and the overwhelming weight of the evidence points to that card being Snape.

Which leads us to one final question, addressed in the next chapter.

What if Snape's never been an enemy of *any* kind? Neither mortal, nor otherwise?

What if all of his unpleasantness toward Harry is part of the trick?

CHAPTER FIFTEEN

Snape Undercover

Your Friendly Host warns, here, that he's about to enter uncharted territory. One of the major strengths of Rowling's story so far is its ability to play fair while seeking wiggle room within its own ambiguities.

Despite everything Your Friendly Host is about to say, there remain any number of possible explanations for everything that's happened so far, including Dumbledore not having even the slightest idea what he's doing.

The following theory is just one of many that fit the available facts, or can be made to fit it with a little hammering of pieces. There are, in fact, just as many reasons to consider it ridiculous, as there are to consider it a real possibility, chief among them the objection that if this is what Rowling has been up to all along, it could very easily come off as a letdown and a terrible cheat. (We'll even get into why.)

Your Friendly Host will go so far as to say that he doesn't believe it himself.

He'll explain that, too.

But this is a big book.

He has plenty of room to just fool around with possibilities, even silly ones.

So here goes.

Think of the miracles we've already seen from wizards, even wizards not quite as great as Dumbledore.

They can fake death.

They can change shape.

They can disguise themselves as other people, well enough to fool others who have known them for years. (Remember, for instance, Barty Crouch's long-term disguise as Mad-Eye Moody.)

Think how convenient tricks like this would be, to forces at war with an enemy as ruthless and as long lived, as Tom Riddle, a.k.a. The Dark Lord, a.k.a. You-Know-Who, a.k.a. Voldemort.

And now, assume, just for the sake of argument, that this is what happened.

In this scenario, James and Lily Potter are what we already know them to be, Dumbledore's allies in the war against Voldemort.

Snape is one of Voldemort's Death Eaters. But then he gets taken out of the game, for any one of several possible reasons. Maybe, as has long been claimed, he sees the error of his ways, and changes sides. Maybe he gets killed. Maybe he just finds himself a place to hide. Whatever happens, he leaves the playing field, under circumstances that make it unlikely he will ever be a problem again.

Dumbledore finds out about this.

(How? Another unknown. Maybe some other spy, as yet unknown to her, brings him the word. Maybe he defeats Snape himself. Or maybe he's just present when Snape melts into a puddle, crying something like, "Aaaarrrrggghhhh! Flobberworms! My Only Weakness!" Whatever. It's enough to say that the real Snape is no longer around, and Dumbledore knows it.)

Dumbledore also determines that Voldemort doesn't know.

And then he sees a possibility.

What if he could make another Snape? One who could infiltrate the Death Eaters, determine their plans, and send regular reports back to Dumbledore, giving the good guys a serious edge?

But for the plan to work, somebody has to become Snape.

He has to take on Snape's mannerisms, Snape's petty grudges, Snape's nastiness, even the mark Snape wears as a member of the Death Eaters.

In short, he has to be every bit as persuasive as Snape as Barty Crouch was as Mad-Eye Moody.

He also has to be a courageous man, who can keep his head while spying on the most evil wizard of the modern world: a man with a long history of getting away with extreme risks, without getting caught and punished.

In short, he has to be Prongs.

Undercover Agent James Potter, at your service.

Why would James Potter do this? After all, he has a wife and a young son to look after. The only possible answer is that he would have to. As future, tragic events will confirm, his family is already on Voldemort's hit list. He can either continue to cower in hiding, or take the fight to the enemy.

Besides, James is every bit the fighter Lupin and Sirius so fondly remember him as being. He's not going to pull a blanket (or even an Invisibility Cloak) over his head when he can do something bold, something that will really hit Voldemort where he lives.

Something that he gets to do while also fiendishly disguising himself as the one kid he loved to make miserable, in the old days.

Of *course* James says yes. His only condition is that Lily, and young Harry, are protected, which Dumbledore is only too happy to do.

Either by himself, or with the help of an accomplished master of Potions, Dumbledore transforms James Potter into a compelling recreation of Severus Snape.

"Snape," in quotes, rejoins Voldemort's forces.

Another of Dumbledore's agents is assigned to pose as James, living under Lily's roof (but not, we hasten to add, as her husband), just to provide more cover for Dumbledore's cunning trick.

And, indeed, the disguised "Snape" proves an excellent spy, sending back all sorts of valuable information that helps turn the tide for the good guys.

Meanwhile, "James" and Lily Potter continue to move from place to place, one step ahead of the Death Eaters.

And then . . . disaster.

A terrible comedy of errors.

"Snape" passes (incomplete) information on to Voldemort, not realizing that it targets his own son.

Pettigrew betrays the Potters to Voldemort.

Voldemort invades the home being used by the Potters, murders the false James, and then turns his murderous attentions on Harry.

Lily dies protecting her son. Harry gets his scar. Voldemort is driven off, a shell of his old self. Sirius takes the blame for betraying the Potters, and is sent to Azkaban. Harry, now famous throughout the entire wizarding world as the only person to survive one of Voldemort's attacks, is retrieved by Hagrid and brought to Dumbledore, who leaves the baby in the care of Uncle Vernon and Aunt Petunia (gee, thanks a lot).

And where is James in all this?

These hours are critical.

Even in this purely hypothetical scenario, Your Friendly Host has no idea how and when James finds out what happened to his family. No doubt he's shattered, inside, by the knowledge that his own mistake led to this. But he doesn't break character as Snape, maybe because the nature of Dumbledore's spell has rendered that difficult or impossible. By the time Dumbledore gets to him, to let him know that Harry's in safe (if thoroughly unpleasant) hands, he's even been arrested, and is in a cell at the Ministry, awaiting the trial that will probably send him straight to Azkaban.

But Dumbledore does get to him, and gives him even more bad news.

It's still not safe for "Snape" to reveal who he really is.

Voldemort is not dead. He's been dealt a serious blow, but he's only been driven back, to nurse his wounds and plot his comeback.

Worse, many of the Death Eaters are still at large, and likely to be let off, on the grounds that they had merely fallen under Voldemort's control. But make no mistake. They're still loyal to the Dark Lord, and still capable of committing terrible crimes in his name.

The second "Snape" reveals that he's really James Potter, he becomes a target again. And so does Harry.

So this is the way things have to be, for now.

James has to continue living as "Snape."

He can avoid imprisonment by telling the Ministry everything he knows about Voldemort's operation. Dumbledore will put in a good word for him, assuring everybody that he switched sides during the conflict. And if anybody remains suspicious of "Snape's" intentions . . . well, Dumbledore, the *Greatest Wizard of the Modern World*, will just have to keep repeating that he trusts "Snape" *implicitly*.

In his everyday life, "Snape" will work for Dumbledore at Hogwarts, a post that will prove especially useful when it comes to keeping an eye on Slytherin, the one House that has always proved the most fertile ground for Voldemort's forces.

If Snape's defection to Dumbledore's forces never happened, and every action he's taken on Harry's behalf is because he's secretly James Potter in disguise, then the entire Harry Potter series becomes about a bully who was right to be a bully because the kid he tormented was every bit the creep his teenage self imagined him to be.

And is J. K. Rowling likely to take that position?

Consider how everything that has happened, up to this point, takes the opposite position, that bullies are a bad thing, and the people worth knowing are those who don't act that way. Uncle Vernon and Aunt Petunia are *wrong* to make Harry feel like an unwanted presence in their home. Dudley is *wrong* to push Harry around at every opportunity. Draco Malfoy is *wrong* to mock and tease the weaker kids. Snape is *wrong* to treat his students so badly. Dolores Umbridge is *wrong* to abuse her power over the students. The various incarnations of Voldemort are *wrong* to use magic as an instrument of terror. The Death Eaters are *wrong* to think that the Strong have the right to wage war on the Weak.

Consider, also, that there has always been a little bit of wiggle-room over whether Trelawney's prophecy actually applied to Harry, or the most put-upon of all Hogwarts students, Neville Longbottom. (That's the half-expected twist that would actually be cool.)

If Harry Potter himself has one virtue that James Potter lacked at his age, it is total contempt for bullies.

Whatever happens, he will not escape *Deathly Hallows* (if in fact he escapes *Deathly Hallows*) without coming to terms with that one glaring difference between himself and his old man.

Whatever happens, he will not escape *Deathly Hallows* (if in fact he escapes *Deathly Hallows*) without also coming to terms with what that means about the relationship between himself and Snape.

In *Order of the Phoenix*, the Sorting Hat breaks from its usual habits, to deliver a mournful song about how, among other things, the great wizards of Gryffindor and Slytherin had once been close friends. It urges the students to unite in the face of the approaching darkness, lest Hogwarts crumble from within.

So maybe that's the key to what's about to happen.

Maybe the climax we're looking for is not "Snape," transforming before Harry's eyes, to offer the revelation, "I've been your father, all along."

Because that would be cheap.

But maybe what we're waiting for is something close to that, something that might lead to the great Houses of Gryffindor and Slytherin becoming allies once again.

Like Harry correcting the one misconception that has led to Snape misjudging him, all these years.

So the key to the whole story is not Snape telling Harry, "I'm your father."

It's Harry telling Snape, "I'm not my father."

CHAPTER SIXTEEN

Voldemort the Pivot

And now it's time to step away from Harry's friends, mentor, and most ambiguous ally, to take a close look at the single most important character in the entire series.

What's that? You disagree?

You think Harry's more important?

Well, he is and he isn't.

He's the most important character because, as we've said more than once, he's the one whose story this is. He's the one who makes the biggest discoveries about himself, the one who is challenged to learn and to grow, and the one who must overcome great odds to survive and even to triumph.

Barring all else, he's the one whose name appears on the cover (though that isn't always a fair way of judging, since we can name any number of books named after minor characters instead of those on stage from beginning to end).

If a character is somebody you know and watch and care about, then, yes, Harry is the most important character.

But he's also a reactive character.

He is what he is because of the world he must face.

Think about it. What happens if we remove Voldemort from the story?

Harry is born to a pair of wizards named James and Lily Potter. He never meets his unpleasant relatives the Dursleys (or, if he does, walks away quickly). He enters Hogwarts just a typical kid of his kind. He never fights Quirrell or the Basilisk, never flees the spiders in the Forbidden Forest, never enters the Triwizard Tournament, never endures the torments of Dolores Umbridge, never fights the Death Eaters at the Ministry of Magic, never joins Dumbledore on the quest for the Horcruxes, never gives up his last year of school in favor of taking the good fight to the enemy.

Remove Voldemort, and the evils committed in his name, and Harry loses everything, even his ambition in life. The Harry we know would like to be an Auror, tracking down evil wizards on behalf of the Ministry. Would he still want that, in the world Voldemort never terrorized? Maybe, but that ambition would certainly lose a great deal of its urgency. In that world, being an Auror would strike Harry as little more than an interesting job.

And that's not all that changes.

If Voldemort never attacks the infant Harry in his crib, the infant Harry never picks up Voldemort's skill at Parseltongue. He doesn't receive a fraction of Voldemort's power. He may have no particular, pressing reason to master the Patronus spell. He loses a great deal of what makes him unique.

Remove Voldemort, and Harry becomes nothing but a talented Quidditch player. The books become a series of novels about the triumphs of a gifted school athlete.

But there's even more than that.

Remove Voldemort, and the evils committed in his name, and Harry's relationship with just about every other character changes beyond recognition.

Oh, he might still befriend Ron. In fact, he might even already know Ron. As Sirius points out in *Order of the Phoenix*, the wizarding community is an awfully small one. It's not hard to imagine little Harry meeting little Ron on social occasions, though there's no special reason to believe that they would have been quite as close, as friends, as they became in the universe we know. Let's give them the benefit of the doubt and say they were destined to be best mates, whatever happened.

But look beyond that.

If not worried about Voldemort getting his hands on it, Dumbledore would have no reason to hide the Sorcerer's Stone in the school. So Quirrell would have no reason to set a cave troll loose in the upstairs corridor. Hermione would never find herself trapped in the bathroom. Ron and Harry would never have to team up to rescue her. Hermione would never have to make up a lie to cover up for them. That moment, which cemented the friendship between the trio we know, would no longer be a part of their shared histories. So Harry and Ron would no longer have any reason to consider her anything but the snotty know-it-all girl who keeps correcting everybody. They might well change their minds a couple of years later (at which point they would likely notice her, for other reasons), but she would not be the special part of their early days at Hogwarts, that she turned out to be in the world we know.

Hagrid might or might not be out of the picture. Remember, Tom Riddle, the future Voldemort, was the one responsible for Hagrid's expulsion. Without Riddle, Hagrid would have graduated and gone on to any number of careers; his half-wizard, half-Giant lineage would not have limited his horizons quite as much as they did in the world we know, and his life path might have taken him far away from Hogwarts. Let us assume for the sake of argument that he remained true to his choice of personal interests and made Care of Magical Creatures his career. Let us also assume that he even ended up teaching it at Hogwarts. He would not have had to visit young Harry, to alert the boy about his magical heritage. He would not have been Harry's guide during the boy's first visit to Diagon Alley. He would not have been Harry's special confidante, but just another member of the faculty, who might or might not have been important to Harry's future life. But that, again, is assuming that he was even at Hogwarts, in the first place.

Remove Voldemort, and the evils committed in his name, and there is no special reason for Dumbledore to consider Harry any more worthy of notice than any of the other young wizards and witches in his care. (Indeed, Dumbledore would probably be spending a lot more time doing his job as headmaster, thus taking care of many of our objections to the man's job performance.) Professor McGonagall wouldn't be taking any special notice of him, either . . . except as a good bet for her House's Quidditch team. Chances are that Lupin would also be out of the picture, as the various circumstances that have turned the Defense Against the Dark Arts professorship into a revolving door would no longer be in play, and Hogwarts would not be so desperate for any warm body to fill the seat that they'd hire anybody, even a werewolf.

Sirius Black would still be around, a good friend to the Potter family who had never sentenced to Azkaban. Harry would grow up liking him a lot, even if their relationship would never quite develop the special tragic weight it did in the world we know. But chances are Harry would not like him any more or less than he'd like that other family friend, Peter Pettigrew, who in this universe would never have had a reason to betray the Potters to anybody. Pettigrew would be nothing more than the funny little man who delighted Harry by transforming into a rat. Nobody would ever have any special reason to suspect Peter of being the sort to sell out his nearest and dearest, since the situation wouldn't have come up.

Harry would never have the galaxy of adult friends and confidantes that he has now. The Weasleys would know him, and possibly even consider him a good kid, but they wouldn't feel the sympathy and protectiveness they have for him now. Mrs. Weasley would never have any reason to declare, in a heated moment, that "'he's as good as'" one of her own children (*Order of the Phoenix* 90). That would be a bit much, given that Harry already had one. There would be no Order of the Phoenix, no circle of experienced wizards to consider Harry a young hero and pivotal element in any protracted, unavoidable war. Dobby the house-elf would have never had any special reason to try to protect Harry, therefore Harry would never have had the opportunity to return the favor by wresting that creature's freedom from the Malfoys. Hermione would have never had the formative experiences that led her to form her well-meaning (and thus far, ineffective) charity, S.P.E.W.

And there's even more than that.

Harry's parents are well off. He's privileged.

And his father has a past as a bully.

Now, we don't know, yet (if we'll ever know) what changed James from the arrogant kid he was to the paragon that everybody seems to remember. Certainly, his brave opposition to Voldemort might have been at least part of it.

But we do know that a cruel sense of humor was at least part of his personality.

We know that our Harry has some of the same tendencies. Just look at the pleasure he takes in baiting Dudley.

Harry's cruel upbringing, in the universe we know, was at least part of what made him a kid who despises bullies on sight.

So who's to say that the Harry of the world that never knew a Voldemort would have been anybody we'd like to know?

That might be overstating things. After all, his mother hated bullies, too, and her influence would have made a huge difference.

But there's still a difference between knowing your mother's code of proper behavior, and believing in it yourself.

So here's the scene that might have been.

It is the beginning of Harry's first year at Hogwarts. The time comes for him to don the Sorting Hat. It examines him, and once again determines that he's suited for either Slytherin or Gryffindor.

Which does he pick?

Well, there's the question.

In the world J. K. Rowling wrote, Harry doesn't want to join Slytherin. Why? Well, in part because he's already made friends with Ron, and wants to be with Ron. But also because he knows that Voldemort was a Slytherin, and has met Draco Malfoy and his cronies and walked away with a horrible first impression of what being a Slytherin means. To the Harry we know, being a Slytherin means being a snob and being a bully, potentially even being evil, and he rejects those qualities so totally that the hat obeys his wishes and places him in Gryffindor, the House that represents all the qualities our Harry admires.

In the world without Voldemort, would he be that adamant about his choice of Houses?

Think about it. This Harry has known privilege since birth. Like our Harry, he's even got a bit of a cruel streak. And Slytherin would not be tarnished, in his eyes, as the House that provided Voldemort with so many recruits, as that reign of terror would no longer be recent history. Morality wouldn't enter into it. It would just be a matter of which place proved the most comfortable.

He might still make it into Gryffindor.

House membership runs in families.

But it could be a very near thing.

If *our* Harry was almost chosen for Slytherin, how much nearer a thing would it be for *this* Harry!

And that brings up even worse possibilities, for the world without Voldemort.

Let's look at one upsetting chain of events.

Imagine for a moment that this Harry becomes a Slytherin.

Our Harry is accustomed to being alone and unpopular. He doesn't like it, but he's been there, and taken it, and emerged able to take it again. So our Harry has more than enough strength to withstand ostracism and peer pressure and stand by whatever he believes to be right. Think about all the times his popularity's taken a kick, even among his fellow Gryffindors, and he's still kept on doing whatever he needed to be doing. This quality of his is most evident during *Chamber of Secrets*, *Goblet of Fire*, and *Order of the Phoenix*, but you can see it exercised at least in passing in all of the books so far.

The Harry of the world without Voldemort would not have spent so many years under the thumb of the Dursleys. He would have lived a fairly stress-free life, soft with love and privilege. Joining Slytherin, he would not have been nearly as prepared for the demands peer pressure would place upon his personality and his value system. He would have learned before long that his crueler and more ruthless qualities were far more valued, in that environment, than his principles and sense of fair play.

So we can just imagine what this Harry would have been like, after a couple of years of palling about with other Slytherins.

We can even imagine him someday cornering Hermione, in the company of his good friends Crabbe and Goyle, to sneer, "*Dirty Mudblood.*"

The world without Voldemort might very well lead to a scene where Ron and Hermione, sitting together in the Great Hall, look across the tables to where a vile, thoroughly unpleasant Harry sits exchanging whispers with Draco Malfoy, and wondering just what evil schemes he's up to.

And if somebody like Tom Riddle, the future Lord Voldemort, came along then, this Harry might have been the first to join him.

Brrrrrrr!

No, it's because of Lord Voldemort that Harry Potter grew up in a place that left him nobody to rely upon but himself. It's because of Lord Voldemort that Harry became a special kid who deserved the close attention of Dumbledore, McGonagall, Lupin, and others. It's because of Lord Voldemort that Harry joined Gryffindor, and because of Lord Voldemort that Harry learned to treasure Hermione. It's because of Lord Voldemort that these books are not about a dull sports star at best and a cruel bully at worst.

In short, it's because of Lord Voldemort that we are where we are now. He's the forge that forms everything important about Harry Potter, both the boy and the bestselling series. Without him, we have nothing.

CHAPTER SEVENTEEN

Voldemort the Villain

ntagonist. Bad Guy. Villain. They all describe Lord Voldemort's place in the Harry Potter saga, without necessarily meaning the same thing. An antagonist doesn't have to be genuinely evil as long as he stands between the hero and his goal. A Bad Guy does have to be evil, but not necessarily formidable, as we all know from any number of stories in which a hero armed with fists or six-guns or laser rifles mows down dozens of them without even raising a sweat.

In most action video games, all those minions you defeat before you get to the level boss are bad guys, but it's hard to distinguish the tenth through twentieth from the twenty-first through thirtieth; they're face-less, by design. Villains are the toughest, and most dangerous of the three, but the very word seems to imply somebody who's larger than life, maybe even larger than death.

119

That fits Voldemort, all right.

But what kind of villain is he?

Well, let's take a brief look at the available categories.

In practice, storytellers in need of villains need to pick theirs from a very short list of basic models.

And it's not so much a list as a continuum.

To the far left we have Villains Who Are Bad Just Because They're Bad. This would include the villain of so many James Bond movies, who is frequently something like an unspeakably wealthy industrialist who has nothing better to do with his money than set off World War III so he can wipe out humanity and live in an underground palace with his mistress, private army, and a large collection of persian cats. Nobody ever asks such a fellow the obvious question, which is just what he believes he would get out of such a lifestyle change, or how he thinks he's ever going to justify such a plan to his Board of Directors. He just wants to do it, that's all. He's bad because he's bad, and there's no reason to even try to understand him.

Then we have Villains Who Are Bad Because They're Crazy. These guys are just plain out of their minds, and operating from motives that would give the rest of us headaches to contemplate. They're just forces of nature, wound up by wonky brain chemistry and pointed at anybody unlucky enough to stand in their way.

Then there are Villains Who Are Bad Because They Want Something. These guys have motivations that make some kind of rational sense, like wanting to steal your stuff. They're bad, they're threats, they're not nice people, but, by God, it is possible to see where they're coming from. Not to mention where they're eventually going.

Then we have Villains Who Are Bad Because They've Been Hurt. These are people who might have been decent enough at one point in their lives, but who have been so grievously wronged, that they've since cast aside all precepts of good and bad in order to indulge themselves in a huge, world-threatening snit. Becoming the Phantom of the Opera, for instance, would make anybody a little bit cranky. It's not only possible to understand people of this ilk, it's also conceivable to feel sorry for them. Because while they may be bad, they do, by God, present their case.

Then we have Villains Who Don't Think They're Bad. Few people really get out of bed in the morning, look out the window, and decide that they're going to be the living embodiment of evil that day. Most people try to do the right thing, even if their version of the right thing is evil by our own standards. This stage would include the despot who wants to take over the world because he believes he can do a better job running it, and the sniper in an enemy army who wants to put a bullet through your heart because he thinks you're threatening his homeland. A villain of this ilk can be just as hissable as the one who twirls his moustache while threatening little Nell. After all, he does just as much damage. Some of the worst monsters in the history of the world were folks who thought they were doing the right thing. But this kind of villain gives us an opportunity denied us by most of the others we've seen: the chance to not only understand, and pity, but also to sympathize.

Move still further down the line and we have Villains Who Know They're Bad But Aren't Happy About It, and Characters Who Aren't Villains But Make Some Hurtful Mistakes Along the Way, but by then we've left Voldemort far behind, so we can return to more appropriate regions and see what all this has to say about him.

The point is that the further you move down the list, the closer you get to people like most of us: guys who do what makes sense to them at the time. Pit bad guys of this kind against heroes who aren't heroes for all the best reasons, and you get complicated stories about complicated people: generally, the best kind.

For the most part, a bad guy who kidnaps the schoolteacher, ties her to the railroad tracks, and rides away snickering for no other reason than *he can* generally doesn't make for very good stories.

And yet what do we have in the Harry Potter novels?

A guy who knows he's evil, who revels in his evil, who is incapable of any kind feelings toward any other human being.

A guy who calls himself the Dark Lord and his disciples the Death Eaters.

He doesn't fool himself into thinking he's morally right.

He knows he's a nasty piece of work.

And that's the way he likes it.

Oh, sure, there are some hints of motivation.

Crazy? Well, he's not exactly a poster boy for mental health.

Does He Want Something? Well, yes. He wants to be the boss.

Has he Been Hurt? Well, yes; his background is even nastier than Harry's, though he seems to have been pretty comfortable in that orphanage. Happy, even, in that the establishment offered him an endless supply of victims to terrorize.

Does He Not Think He's Bad? Not quite. He knows he's bad. (Why else would he style himself a "Dark Lord"?) But as far as he's concerned, scouring the earth of Mudbloods and Muggles is a good thing. If he can torture and kill as many of his enemies as possible, in the meantime, well, then, why not? This is not a guy who'll deny himself the opportunity to have fun.

But all that is really window dressing.

At heart, he's the flattest kind of Villain, the kind Who's Bad Because He's Bad.

And that's the toughest kind to write well because he exists only to get the story rolling. You can never really get to know a guy like this, even if you have a helpful wizard like Dumbledore who can cue up all of his formative experiences on the wizard DVD deck known as a Pensieve. He's just plain evil because he's evil. You can only hope that he gets arrested or blown up or tossed into the volcano before he does too much damage, because chances are that the story will never be about him, just about stopping him.

And yet, against all odds, he's one of the Great Villains of modern fiction. Why is that?

Why is he worth more than a nickel when there's so little to him?

Well, for the best possible demonstration, let's perform a total lobotomy on the Harry Potter universe and see what the stories would be like if Voldemort and the Death Eaters were all our heroes had to worry about.

> *We join Harry and his friends at the beginning of another bright, sunshiny day at Hogwarts. They walk all together in a clump—Ron worrying about his homework, Hermione scolding him for not starting it earlier the night before, Neville tripping over his robes, and Harry basking in the company of his friends. Then, suddenly, somebody screams! It's Voldemort and the Death Eaters, flying low over the forest! They're attacking the school! We see Voldemort himself, hurling bolts of pure destruction at the school building, cackling that this time he will triumph for sure. Why isn't the faculty doing something? Look, they're all unconscious! They've been put to sleep by some kind of magical spell! It's up to Harry and his friends! Harry's eyebrows knit in determina-*

tion. "To the brooms!" he orders. Harry's gang leaps to the school's defense, hurling Defensive magic against the attacking Death Eaters. Harry is of course the one who gets to fight Voldemort, and they exchange mutual taunts that range from Voldemort's usual "You Will Die!" to Harry's brilliant riposte, "Not This Time, Lizard-Face!" Meanwhile, Hermione figures out a magic spell that wakes up the faculty. As Hagrid hurls a giant cornice stone at the evil Lucius Malfoy, knocking him off his broom, Voldemort realizes that his team is now sorely outnumbered. "Curse you, Harry Potter!" he cries, as the robed villains all turn tail and fly away, vowing to return. Dumbledore fondly praises Harry for saving the day yet again. Harry says it was nothing. Hedwig makes a comical chirp and falls off his perch. Everybody laughs in unison.

If the structure of that awful paragraph sounds at all familiar, that's deliberate: it was written to resemble a fifteen-minute animated cartoon.

Your Friendly Host is well aware that some of these are actually good, so you don't have to write him with examples of ones you like. He was aiming for the worst of the worst; the ones where every episode is essentially the same story, and the adventures were bloodless not just because they contained no gore but because nobody in them had substance of any kind. Slice any of these people in half and they won't bleed, because they have no blood vessels. They're just white fluffy sameness, like baked potatoes.

Reduce the Harry Potter universe to its absolute minimum and it's actually a fairly accurate adaptation. Some of Harry's younger fans (including those who follow neither the books nor the movies, but do bug their parents for the toys), would probably be delighted. Many would come to think of this fifteen-minute cartoon as "their" Harry.

No doubt there's a parallel universe somewhere where the books are not quite as popular as they are here, and their creator does not enjoy the degree of power J. K. Rowling has here, and the books do not fall into the hands of the committed, talented, and respectful filmmakers they do here: where as a result audiences do not get the big-budget, more-or-less faithful Hollywood adaptations our Harry received, but instead cartoons much like this, which can be watched and made into toys and gradually abandoned to space-filler on some obscure cable channel.

And yet, notice something.

The stupid dialogue aside, is any of it actually out of character with the people we know?

Would Harry, Ron, Hermione, Neville, Dumbledore, and Hagrid *not* act this way?

Most importantly, is there anything in that awful, awful, *awful* paragraph that does not sound like Voldemort?

You could argue that he's never been the type to come at his enemies head-on, with full frontal assaults. You could say that he also employs on spies, and sabotage, and assassinations, and psychological warfare. This is very much true, especially in those early books before *Goblet of Fire* where he's a disembodied force popping up out of diaries and the back of random heads. In those early volumes, he doesn't have the resources to attempt any attack quite as bold as the one in our cartoon scene; and were he to attempt one anyway, Dumbledore would have squashed him like a bug by chapter two, each time. But that full-scale charge isn't out of character either. Remember the Death Eaters raiding the Ministry in *Order of the Phoenix*, or the subsequent assault on Hogwarts itself in *Half-Blood Prince*. Seriously, this isn't all that much of a stretch.

Clearly, if Voldemort's a great villain, as Your Friendly Host believes him to be, then that's not because of his motives, or his personality, or even his tactics.

If he's a great villain, it may not even have anything to do with him.

It may, in fact, have more to do with the difficulty of mounting an effective fight against him.

Because this is one key fact the Harry Potter books recognize.

In any epic battle between Good and Evil, Evil gets its act together while Good is still putting on its shoes.

Harry Potter doesn't get to run into the headmaster's office and yell, "Golly Gee, Professor! Voldemort's on the loose again!" The universe he inhabits is more complex than that, and just knowing the danger isn't the same as being able to get people to listen, or even knowing who to trust. The entire story of Harry Potter hinges on its young hero never knowing where to tread, who to rely upon, when to keep his head down, or when to stand up for himself. This is most obvious during *Order of the Phoenix*, where the Ministry considers Voldemort's return a fraud, cooked up as part of a power grab by Dumbledore. In that book, mounting a defense against Voldemort is dangerous for reasons that have nothing to do with the Dark Lord himself. It makes Harry and his allies targets of a government which would rather deny the facts and protect its own existence. As a result, the shifting landscape provides Harry with his old enemy Professor Snape, whose hatred of our hero complicates Harry's need to learn from him; Cornelius Fudge, a politician intent on protecting his own power who uses the press and Dolores Umbridge to destroy Harry's credibility as a witness to Voldemort's rebirth; and Umbridge again, who strangles her Defense Against the Dark Arts classes in theory, to prevent the kids from ever receiving the practical knowledge the Ministry considers a threat to its own power. Even in *Half-Blood Prince*, when Voldemort's return has been proven to the Ministry's satisfaction, the ground continues to shift. Dumbledore is still suspect. The wrong people are still being arrested. The Ministry remains less interested in stopping Voldemort than in putting the best political spin on events.

All of this while the world continues to slide over the edge of the cliff.

Voldemort's Evil is absolute. There's no possible use in debating it. The dude is bad, bad, bad, bad, bad. And anybody who aids and abets him is also bad, bad, bad, bad, bad, bad. The situation's getting worse every day. There's no time to lose.

But that doesn't mean anybody agrees on what to do about him.

Even the people we like don't necessarily agree about it.

In *Order of the Phoenix*, Sirius thinks it's just great that the kids are starting the illegal Defense Against the Dark Arts classes. Ron's mom thinks it's an unnecessary risk that will only get them in trouble with the Ministry.

Hermione, who thinks out everything, even sees it both ways.

Who's right?

They all are.

But the ground is constantly shifting.

There's no way to know, for sure.

It's not like it helps to seek advice. In the Harry Potter books, every authority figure can be right, wrong, or some combination thereof.

Nor can Harry always trust bad guys to always do the wrong thing. We've already had cause to question Snape's bad intentions. But there's also Black, who turned out to be a loving godfather indeed. And Draco Malfoy, who delights in the idea of being an evil icon like his father, but who also memorably finds out, in *Half-Blood Prince*, that there's something he cannot bring himself to do.

And as for the people whose examples he should want to emulate: Dumbledore may be guilty of too much trust; Hagrid isn't always great at spotting danger; Sirius Black is bored and reckless; James Potter himself, the hero who is held out to Harry as an icon and as a role model, may have feet of clay.

What can Harry do?

Who can he trust?

Should he listen to this one, or that one?

Should he stay low? Do something bold?

Wait?

He can't afford to wait.

But he can't afford to do the wrong thing, either.

So maybe he should wait.

But maybe he doesn't dare.

And again, the ground continues to shift.

There are even indications that the magical world isn't that absolute a contrast. As early as *Chamber of Secrets*, we begin to learn that it rests on the slavery of house-elves and the exploitation or extermination of other magical creatures. By *Order of the Phoenix*, we learn about wizards killing off all the Giants in Britain. These are the people Hagrid tries to enlist, for Dumbledore's side. And these are the people the Death Eaters are after, in a different way.

Circles within circles.

More shifting ground. The introduction of moral complexity. Good, revealed as not very Good at all.

The only certainty is that Voldemort *is out there*, his evil undeniable, his malice a proven fact, his crimes an ongoing history, his final confrontation with Harry a matter of established prophecy. That's the only thing Harry can be sure of.

And that, dear reader, is why Voldemort's such a great villain.

Not just because he shows up with his lizard-face and his magic wand and his army of worshippers, eager to destroy everything Harry holds dear. That much is true of the cartoon-Voldemort we saw a few pages ago, and he's a big fat generic nothing. You'll forget that Voldemort by tomorrow's lunch.

But, Voldemort's long shadow . . . that's something else.

That has changed everything.

It's filled the world with uncertainty. Nobody knows what to do about him. Nobody knows what Harry should do and nobody knows what the Ministry should do. And while the Ministry continues to worry about its own power and the proper public relations response to the problem, and while Dumbledore's people find themselves continuing to bog down in politics, the danger continues to grow direr every day.

Because Voldemort suffers no such uncertainties.

He is what he is.

His mind will never change.

And while the good guys are stumbling about, in frantic debate with one another, he knows exactly what he wants. . . .

CHAPTER EIGHTEEN

Voldemort the Crime Boss

Y es. We know. Harry gets two chapters. Hagrid gets two chapters. Ron and Hermione get two chapters. Dumbledore and Snape get two chapters.

And Voldemort gets three?

Just what's the deal here? Is Your Friendly Host afraid of Death Eaters visiting his house in the middle of the night? Is he perhaps a Death Eater himself, with insufficient power to give the Dark Lord the world, but with just enough influence over the words on these pages to hand him that all-important extra slot on the table of contents?

Your Friendly Host must claim innocence, and will continue to do so even as he rubs nervously at the mark on his arm.

No, in truth, this chapter is not about Voldemort at all, but needs to include him because his nature is so inextricably linked to the nature of the people who follow him.

We need to ask about those guys.

Because, seriously.

Remember that cartoon version of Harry and Voldemort, just a few pages ago? Here's another one:

> *Suddenly the door to the Ministry chambers vanished in a brilliant burst of light. The dozens of illustrious witches and wizards, all gathered for an important conference on magical policy, all turned their heads as one, and saw the unpleasant Hogwarts student Tom Riddle, now hideously transformed into the evil Lord Voldemort, the most evil wizard who ever lived. "You have a choice!" Voldemort cried. "You can follow me, or die!" He brandished his wand in emphasis, but long before he could utter the Cruciatis or Avada Kedavra Curses, dozens of other wizards from all corners of the room had all gestured with theirs, and an entire rainbow of other curses and hexes had all converged on the intruder, transfixing him, petrifying him, and transforming him into a creature equally toad, newt, rabbit, teacup, Jelly bean, guinea pig, goldfish, paramecium, slime mold, flobberworm, and screwt. The thing squirmed for all of two seconds before the combination of its own irreconcilable biology and the heel of Albus Dumbledore reduced it to a thin red paste.*
>
> *"Good thing he was alone," Dumbledore remarked later. "A nutter like that, if he'd managed to get himself some followers, might have caused some real trouble."*

Obviously, Lord Voldemort, the lone wolf villain who can't get anybody to listen to him, is dangerous only to a limited degree. Assume exceptional cunning on his part and he'll kill a few people here and a few people there before public pressure, and the dedicated efforts of talented Aurors, leads to him being tracked down and imprisoned for his crimes. Far from a multi-volume epic involving hundreds of speaking characters, and many lesser crimes and conspiracies over seven years and thousands of pages . . . what you have instead is a one-hour episode of *Law and Order: Magical Crimes Unit.*

But that, as we all know, is not the Lord Voldemort we ended up with.

Our Lord Voldemort is a dark charismatic leader, with entire legions of dedicated followers who worship him as something more than human.

His influence extends to every level of wizarding society, sabotaging any efforts against him, terrifying the innocent in their beds, and tempting the cowardly and weak at heart to betray their own friends in the hope that currying favor will allow them to survive the world to come.

As a result, he has people who hide him when he's infirm, who perform the errands he considers beneath him, and who have no difficulty carrying out his every whim, even if that does include the assassinations of young children.

What a difference an army makes!

But that leads to a very pressing question.

Just how did this guy ever get anybody to follow him?

The first thing we notice is that it can't be just because of his winning personality.

Oh, he's charming enough. But it's a shallow charm. He can fake human warmth, but genuine human connection is not one of the man's gifts. He will pretend friendship for some and even declare his great joy at seeing others, but that surface personality is reptilian at best. (His current physical appearance makes that quite literal.) The malice drips from almost every word he speaks, and even the people who believe in him demonstrate, with their own obsequiousness in his presence, that they know he's capable of turning on them at any time.

This phenomenon is best illustrated by one of those scenes you so often find in books and movies, so over-the-top that it never rings true even in stories that are pitched at the fantastic level in the first place. The villain's minion delivers bad news of some kind, perhaps details of our brave hero's latest impossible escape from a death trap. The villain cries, "What!?," and kills the messenger in a fit of rage, therefore proving just how crazy he is.

You know. You've seen that scene any number of times. You've read it in books and seen it in movies. And most of the time you just go along with it, because it's done in a fun way or because it would be too much trouble to argue.

But sometimes, that scene catches you in a skeptical mood.

And instead of just waiting for what happens next, you find yourself arguing. "Oh, come on," you say. "That was uncalled for. What about all of the thugs in the room? Don't they care about the guy who just got killed? Don't they ever ask themselves, 'Wow, why am I working for this crazy person who's so out of control that he's likely to strike me dead the next time I forget an item on his grocery list?' Wouldn't they say, 'You know, it's not worth whatever he pays me if I might not be alive to spend it?' Wouldn't they say, 'Okay. That does it. I'm not even gonna quit. But when I get in my car tonight, I'm going to keep driving?'"

> *"I used to work for Doctor Sardonicus," Bill said. "But then came the day he got mad and dropped the whole Accounting Department into that pit of ravenous Piranhas. I mean, I worked with some of those guys, and that was really over the top. I don't need that kind of treatment in the workplace."*

Come on. You know you've wondered about this, at one time or another. But here's the deal.

You only find that hard to believe because you're sane.

You're not in the employ of a monster.

You haven't had months or years for that situation to gradually come to define "normal" in your head.

So you encounter that scene where the thugs watch as their co-worker is murdered by their boss, and you think it's ridiculous.

But here's the thing.

It may be ridiculous, but as a storytelling convention it makes more sense than you think.

There's a real-life phenomenon called Stockholm Syndrome, named after a bank robbery where hostages were taken. The standoff lasted for days. The robbers beat their prisoners, and threatened to kill them, and gave them good reason to fear for their lives. But in between moments of brutality they doled out small kindnesses, like minor compliments or polite thank you's for obeying orders.

In that context, people can feel ridiculously grateful for a cup of water, or permission to go to the bathroom.

By the time the police took the robbers into custody, some of the hostages were reported to be deeply sympathetic to the people who imprisoned them. It was even said that a couple of the women agreed to marry their captors, though this has been chalked up to a mistranslation of the police report, when the story made its way to other countries. In truth, the captives in that case may not have experienced Stockholm

Syndrome at all, but the phenomenon has been observed many times since, in kidnappings and other hostage situations.

We can certainly apply it to any number of real-life situations where people worked for monsters.

For instance, the American gang boss Al Capone threw a fancy dinner party where, for dessert, he surprised two of his guests by carrying out his intention to beat them to death with a baseball bat.

What kind of idiot would want to work for that guy?

The Ugandan dictator Idi Amin threw lavish soirees, impressing everybody around him with his warmth and generosity. Everybody had a great time at his celebrations. Everybody also knew that whenever he grew unhappy with somebody, that person disappeared and was never heard from again. Unsurprisingly, people went out of their way to make him happy. Your Friendly Host has seen footage of a party at Amin's mansion, where he challenged members of his cabinet to a race across the pool. Everybody dives in at the same time. Amin turns out to be exactly as good a swimmer as you expect him to be, which is to say, as good as any other fat man who spends most of his time riding a desk. Some of the people racing him are younger and clearly in much better shape than he is. But they're all so determined to let him win that one stops swimming at the halfway point, and two others veer off in other directions rather than risk accidentally touching the finish line. It's so obvious it's pathetic. Amin crows, "I won!" And sure, he did. You always win contests like that if everybody else is scared to death of irritating you.

What kind of idiot would want to work for that guy?

The Soviet Dictator Josef Stalin ruled his country with an iron fist. His advisors enjoyed a degree of power close to his, and all the perks that the Soviet Union was able to provide. But they also lived in fear, because every once in a while he decided that somebody close to him was getting too powerful, or too popular, or too *anything other than him* . . . and that person would go away, either executed in secret or exiled to the hellish prisons known as Gulags that were very much in Azkaban's class.

What kind of idiot would want to work for that guy?

Organized crime gangs, throughout the world, all operate under the same model. If the boss likes you, you get lots and lots and lots of goodies. You may be rich and you may be almost as powerful as the big guy. But there's a price. You have to keep him happy. And there may be no telling what will keep him happy. The day after he claps you on the back and says that you're the one person he can trust, he may hear a rumor that you're holding out money or planning a takeover or talking to the police. The same guy who called you his best friend yesterday may be showing up at your front door with a gun tomorrow. You have to live with it. That's the deal you made.

But who would want to work for those guys?

Doesn't anybody in any of these situations ever look at what they're living with, and say, "You know, this really isn't the safest way to live?"

Well, yeah. It happens.

People quit or run away or join the other side or take a shot at the boss.

That's why so many of these monsters spend so much time worrying about the loyalty of the people who work for them.

That's why they go over the top when they feel they must make an example.

But you'd be surprised how many people just go on working for them, taking every fresh mistreatment as just another reason to be loyal.

Endure that kind of treatment long enough, and you may find yourself grateful for just being allowed to live.

Goblet of Fire is clearest on this subject, after the Port Key in the hedge maze transports Harry and Cedric Diggory to the Riddle Family crypt. Peter Pettigrew sacrifices some of his own flesh to restore Voldemort to power.

Is Voldemort grateful? The word doesn't really apply to him. He doesn't feel grateful to anybody, for anything. But he doesn't even pretend to be. Instead, he reminds Pettigrew how badly he's fallen down on the job. Pettigrew cowers, thinking that he's about to be punished. Voldemort makes him cringe, then gives him a reward. The sniveling Pettigrew proves to be ridiculously grateful.

Voldemort treats the rest of his Death Eaters the same way. They obey his summons. Again, he questions their loyalty before welcoming them back into the fold.

Their fear of him is so great that their loyalty is only cemented when he declines to punish them as horribly as they know he can.

Let's take a look at Pettigrew, in particular. He may be the most pathetic villain in the Harry Potter universe. Voldemort has an excuse, in that he's Evil Incarnate. Pettigrew is just a worm . . . or, given the appropriate nature of his Animagus talents, a rat. He's capable of nothing but hiding in the shadow of figures more powerful than himself. That's why he spends so many years in hiding as Ron Weasley's pet rat, Scabbers (and, seriously, people: ewwwww). And that's how we see him in *Order of the Phoenix*, hanging around the much more popular James Potter, watching with open adoration as James shows off for his benefit.

This happens in the very same scene where we learn that James spent his school years making Snape's life miserable, a revelation that shakes our respect for James Potter's memory almost as much as it shakes Harry's.

The bullying of Snape may be all you remember of that scene.

But take another look and you'll see that Snape is not the only one being bullied.

Pettigrew's worship of James's power is so pathetic, and James Potter's clear enjoyment of that worship so self-serving, that it emerges as just another example of a strong kid taking advantage of a weaker one.

James shows off for Pettigrew, soaking in his admiration. A bored Sirius wonders if Pettigrew is about to wet himself with excitement.

They're both mocking Pettigrew, in different ways. They're taunting him and hurting this kid who's supposed to be their friend, showing just enough friendship toward him that he's left grateful for their attention.

It's not a healthy relationship.

It's based on power.

And the young Pettigrew is just the type to respond to it.

The power he gets from hanging out with stronger people is the only power he will ever have.

Now flash forward a few years, to Voldemort's reign of terror. The relationship based on power is threatened by the arrival of a bigger and hungrier fish. Pettigrew, who the Potters imagined their friend, sells out to the more threatening bully. He will later tell himself that he had no choice. Sirius and Lupin will coldly inform him, in *Goblet of Fire*, that he did. He could have died to keep the Potters safe.

But that's not even the real point, when you're talking about a personality like his. The point is that the safety of the Potters barely even entered into it. The feeling of power a Pettigrew can only achieve in the shadow of somebody with power is.

The truth is: Voldemort probably didn't even have to threaten him all that much.

For Pettigrew, it was like getting a raise.

Now, multiply Pettigrew by hundreds. Or thousands.

Or millions.

In our own recent history, entire countries have gone mad this way, with entire populations throwing away their own understanding of right and wrong, because it was easier to just chant "yes, sir" to the bullies in power.

This is equally true of the wizarding world, which has any number of weak-willed who will join Voldemort only because he's the guy who's best at throwing his weight around.

No doubt there are any number of others who won't take a stand either way, until they see which side is about to win. We won't know for certain until *Deathly Hallows*, but Your Friendly Host is pretty sure that Dolores Umbridge, for one, acts out of what she considers to be loyalty to Cornelius Fudge and the Ministry. But he's also pretty sure that if Voldemort seized power tomorrow he would have absolutely no trouble hiring her as one of his most trusted aides. And not just because *she's* as cruel as he is, but because everything *he's* about echoes everything she's about. She would simper and thrill at the mere thought of being so close to somebody who was so clearly in charge.

Again, multiply her by thousands.

Or millions.

All of this seems to explain why people follow Voldemort after he's become the fearsome creature he is, but not why they join up with him in the first place.

And the answer is: for pretty much the same reason.

Why does young Pettigrew hang out with James Potter? Because he can't be James Potter. The best he can accomplish is being close to James Potter.

How does Voldemort start building his base as a student in Slytherin?

By exploiting the same kind of feeling.

We know from *Half-Blood Prince* that Tom Riddle's cruelty and contempt for others were already major parts of his personality by the time Dumbledore found him. We know, for instance, that he had nothing but disdain for anybody he could bully or push around. To his perspective, people he could terrorize were less than human. It's therefore no big leap for him to hate Muggles and those he would call Mudbloods—even though he's not a pure-blood himself. (His hatred of his own family is, of course, a large part of what makes him what he is.)

But what happens when he joins the wizarding world, much the same way Harry did?

He discovers that he's not the only person who feels this way.

He discovers a wide streak of bigotry, cutting through all of the wizarding world.

He discovers, too, that his viciousness will make him a role model, of sorts, to people who like that kind of thing.

He discovers that speaking out about what he believes will make him friends.

He discovers that some of those friends are people with influence, who will nevertheless look up to him, and do his bidding.

He discovers that once he makes one or two of those people his slaves, by vividly demonstrating his own willingness to punish them for not following his every wish, there's no bottom to it. His demands can grow more imperious, more insane. And the definition of sanity, among his crowd, will shift, to accommodate him. There comes a day when he turns to the person next to him and makes a demand so outrageous that only a year earlier the same person would have told him to drop dead. Instead, the order is obeyed at once.

And the people who witness it give up a little bit of their humanity and say, yes, of course, we have to obey him when he makes a request like that, because he's who he is.

The ground shifts.

He only needs a few, to start.

After that, the rest start falling in line.

To join him. Or to fight him.

Or to die.

CHAPTER NINETEEN

Dolores Umbridge: Fear Itself

This one's special. Even in a world terrorized by Lord Voldemort, Dolores Umbridge stands alone. Aside from Aragog, who merely sees him as a convenient bag of calories, she is the only deadly enemy in Harry's life whose murderous intentions toward him seem to owe nothing to Lord Voldemort's machinations, the only monster who represents the so-called legitimate rulers of the wizarding world and not the Dark Lord who seeks to overthrow them.

Politics was always present in Harry's world, complicating his efforts to survive whatever horrid menace stalks the halls of Hogwarts each semester. It's certainly a major factor in the back-story. But it's Dolores Umbridge who teaches him that the real danger is being found politically inconvenient. It is Dolores Umbridge who sends Dementors after him, then persecutes him for "lying" when he reports what happened to him;

Dolores Umbridge who tries to make his life at Hogwarts intolerable; and Dolores Umbridge who, with her Masters at the Ministry, dedicates herself to destroying Harry's credibility with his fellow students. It is Dolores Umbridge who teaches Harry that not all enemies stand on the other side of the battlefield, Dolores Umbridge who teaches him that some enemies fly the same flag you do but will do anything they can to eliminate everything it stands for. It is, in short, Dolores Umbridge who teaches Harry about fascism.

Heavy stuff.

And not at all what we would normally expect from a series of children's books.

But J. K. Rowling is telling an epic story here, not just one about a battle between good and evil, but one about all the shades of gray on both sides. Thus we have Voldemort minions who balk at murder and good guys who were bullies in high school and wise old wizards who make mistakes and, in the form of Dolores Umbridge, a monster who commits vile crimes against children in the name of a government that has come to care for nothing but protecting its own grip on power. She no doubt believes in everything she's doing. She believes it so much that whenever she makes up a lie to smear Harry she comes to believe in the lie as well. She would certainly argue with anybody who dared to suggest that this made her as evil, in her own way, as Voldemort. After all, she's destroying lives for a *good cause*. She's terrorizing a school to *keep order*. Even her torture of Harry is really being done *for the good of the community*.

She honestly believes this.

At least, it looks like she honestly believes this.

We have no way of knowing what we may learn about her in *Deathly Hallows*.

She may well turn out to be a Death Eater, infiltrating the Ministry.

We hope not.

Since the evil she represents is very real, even in our own world . . . and not just the plot of a super-villain . . . any revelation explaining her wickedness as the doings of a mere Voldemort minion would strike us as a downer and a cheat.

You don't need that kind of cop-out to understand Dolores Umbridge.

Fascism is when a government treats the people as a threat to its own grip on power. Sometimes it occurs when a country perceives a menace, like spies or terrorists, who provides the people in charge with an excuse to clamp down on its citizens in the guise of protecting them.

These menaces are not always real. Sometimes they're imaginary or overstated or deliberately made up by the government. Sometimes they're whistle-blowers. The very people who stand up to point out very serious problems can be painted as the threat themselves. This is what happens in *Order of the Phoenix.* Voldemort is real. He has returned. But Fudge doesn't believe this. He suspects Dumbledore of using Harry to prepare a power grab. So Dumbledore, and anybody connected to him, is perceived as an enemy.

Umbridge's subsequent persecution of the school sounds crazy. But Rowling bases it on many incidents in real life. Schools and Universities have long been seen as dangerous places where kids are taught to challenge the people in charge. They've always had to deal with the tug of war between young people who have the right to ask questions about the world they'll be running someday, and the current bosses who believe that they should be taught nothing but loyalty. In extreme cases, the people in charge attack the very idea of education. There was one very terrible group of people called the Khmer Rouge, who upon taking power in Cambodia began killing anybody foolish enough to admit to having an education. That included doctors, lawyers, and teachers. If you had a diploma, you were dead.

The classic example in the United States is of course campus activism, which reached a peak in the 1960s. The government of the time was correct to fear some of these activities; after all, some organizations that recruited on American campuses saw no problem with practicing violence. Unfortunately, the peaceful activists of the time were also right to distrust the government, which had infiltrated them and was happy to urge them into committing crimes. There was bloodshed on both sides. In one infamous incident out of many, National Guardsmen opened fire on protestors at Kent State, killing four. Even today, long after the fires of that decade have cooled, we still argue over the lessons we teach our students, with people on both sides of the political spectrum outdoing the other in condemning teachers who teach the "wrong" lessons.

Crazy? Yes. But perfectly believable.

In scary times, the Ministry of Magic would naturally see Hogwarts as a potential source of new enemies.

And it's no accident that the measures taken by Dolores Umbridge make Hogwarts less a school than a prison, less interested in teaching its students than keeping them under strict control at all times.

The first indication of her plans comes on opening day, when she hijacks the banquet to make a turgid speech about "a new era of openness, effectiveness, and accountability, intent on preserving what ought to be preserved, perfecting what needs to be perfected, and pruning wherever we find practices that ought to be prohibited" (*Order of the Phoenix* 213-214). As with any number of speeches by real-life leaders, the dangerous passages are buried in a sea of indigestible rhetoric. In this case, a promise of "openness" begins the very same sentence that warns about mysterious, and sinister, new prohibitions.

Most Hogwarts students, with the notable exception of Hermione, who again demonstrates her knack of understanding what's really going on, perceive Umbridge as a boring old blowhard, and fail to pay any attention.

But the density of Umbridge's rhetoric is the very point. Because if she spoke her intent in plain language, she'd enflame opposition at the very start. Her true purpose, here, is not to introduce all of her changes right away, but to get a foot in the door.

The thing is, it's perfectly possible for freedom to fail overnight, but it usually takes an invading army. More dangerous fascist movements proceed with caution, introducing their abuses one step at a time. Supposedly, if you toss a frog in a pot of boiling water, it will react to the sudden agony by jumping out if it can. Put the same frog in a pot of room-temperature water and increase the heat by one degree every ten minutes and the frog won't realize the trouble it's in even as it starts to cook.

Professor Umbridge understands this, which is one reason she introduces her changes in the form of a series of nested abuses, each one couched in the most beneficial language possible. It's worth noting that if any one of her actions met with effective resistance, the next would not be possible, which is one reason why the earliest are so couched in language nobody's going to listen to.

This is absolutely true of her stewardship of the Defense of the Dark Arts class, which is no longer the hands-on training of previous years, but a "carefully structured, theory-centered, Ministry-approved course," (*Order of the Phoenix* 239), which she has re-structured to discourage students from obtaining any practical knowledge. Umbridge couches this as "'theoretical knowledge . . . more than sufficient to get you through your examination, which, after all, is what school is all about.'" (*Order of the Phoenix* 243). (School should be about learning, not passing tests. Don't get Your Friendly Host started on certain real world developments.) What Umbridge offers is not so much an education as the pretense of one, aimed at pumping out students incapable of challenging anybody. When the class, which knows that it's being shortchanged, protests, Umbridge first places tight controls on who's allowed to speak, then attacks her predecessors as "'irresponsible'" and (in the case of Lupin) "'dangerous half-breeds'" (*Order of the Phoenix* 243). Harry's own objections result in him being placed under a detention that (he soon finds out) includes Umbridge's own special form of torture.

It's Professor McGonagall who warns Harry of the true danger he's in. "'Do you really think this is about truth or lies? It's about keeping your head down and your temper under control!'" (*Order of the Phoenix* 249).

Exactly.

Umbridge has made it too dangerous to ask questions.

The outrages continue and grow more, not less, reminiscent of the way things work in the real world. Harry's friends are pressured to drop him. The newspaper overflows with stories attacking Harry's credibility: stories that seem to have been written at government behest, by reporters who just take down what they're being told. Those who defend Harry or Dumbledore, or question the motives of the Ministry, are themselves scapegoated: Madam Marchbanks, whose protests appear in one news story, is cited as having "alleged links to subversive goblin groups." Hermione is punished for expressing an opinion that conflicts with the one she's read in her textbook.

Umbridge is given the new office of Inquisitor, and tasked to question every member of the Hogwarts faculty, prior to a planned purge. She uses this opportunity to direct her full wrath at anybody suspected of sympathizing with Dumbledore, and when she cannot find evidence, has no qualms about manufacturing it (at one point filing a negative report about Hagrid, that she maliciously concocts on the spot).

There is a real world name for this, too. It's called an Enemies List. It condemns not only those who oppose the administration, but also those associated with them. Given full power, an Enemies List can blight the existences of anybody unlucky enough to even know somebody listed there. In Stalin's Soviet Union, and Saddam Hussein's Iraq, people associated with others on such lists could be hauled off to prison on the flimsiest of pretexts. If they were lucky, they merely suffered financial hardships and official harassment. If they were unlucky, they were killed.

Enemies Lists have also been, unfortunately, in common use within the United States. In the 1950s, it was dangerous just to be casual friends with people Senator Joe McCarthy had included on his list of communists. In the 1970s, President Richard Nixon had another Enemies List, of people who had opposed his administration in any way. In recent years, Enemies Lists have become even more prominent, with many political pundits (on both sides) using them as the basis of unrestrained attacks on those whose opinions conflict with their own. Accusations of treason are flung again and again against the same short list of names, so often that before long anything they might have to say is considered crazy or unpatriotic regardless of the points being made.

The dangerous thing, of course, is that there is no bottom line. The more repressive a society becomes, the more repressive it tries to become. There's a steady progression from shutting somebody up to shutting him away, from discouraging certain thoughts to outlawing them, from curtailing some rights to taking them away. All tyrannies, however long-established, exist in a constant state of experimentation, as they continue to discover what they can get away with next. In Hogwarts, under Umbridge, the outrages that here climax with Hagrid under siege are just the beginning of a process that, if allowed to go unopposed, will only get worse. Readers can only shudder at the prospect on just how terrible Hogwarts would have become were Umbridge allowed to run it unopposed for another five years, or ten, or twenty. Who would be allowed to attend? What would they be taught? And what would the faculty do, to any students who dared to think inconvenient thoughts at inconvenient times? If Umbridge already engages in torture now, what would she be willing to do in a decade?

Terrifying questions.

But tyrannies fall.

And the reason they fall, is that people oppose them.

In *Order of the Phoenix*, that opposition takes two forms.

First, at the urging of Ron and Hermione, Harry recruits a group of trusted students for his own illicit Defense Against the Dark Arts classes. They are risking their futures to learn that which the state, with its current fascistic excesses, would prefer them not to learn.

The difference between their situation, and that of similar students struggling under repressive regimes in the real world, is only that the magical nature of Harry's universe makes the nature of their "crime" literal.

Because these illicit lessons *empower* them. These illicit lessons make them *dangerous*. These illicit lessons give them *what they need to survive*. These illicit lessons free them from the empty rote-learning Fudge has mandated to keep them *harmless*.

The other major rebellion, a series of spectacular stunts performed by the practical jokers Fred and George, is just as influential. They succeed in making Umbridge look ridiculous, and once caught, reject her authority over them outright, flying off to begin their adult lives while offering major discounts on their practical joke equipment to any Hogwarts students to "'swear they're going to use our products to get rid of this old bat.'" (*Order of the Phoenix* 675). The groundswell of public admiration for these pranks makes it increasingly difficult for Umbridge to maintain her position as unquestioned authority figure. After their departure, pranks continue, and Umbridge is driven ragged trying to maintain her composure in the face of steadily increasing chaos.

And this, too, has a precedent in reality. Nothing hurts an established power figure more than being made to look ridiculous.

One of the most famous pranks of the kind was the Boston Tea Party, when colonists opposed to the tax policies of the British crown boarded a ship dressed as Indians and poured its entire shipment of tea into the harbor. In the United States, this incident is taught anew to entire generations of schoolchildren, but (alas) almost always in summary only, with little attention given to explaining exactly why the stunt worked. After all, if the point had only been the mere destruction of the tea, there would have been any number of other ways to do it. The ship could have been set afire, or made to sink. But dressing like Indians—a tactic never intended to shift blame, but rather to echo the stereotype of *noble savage*—turned the Tea Party into street theatre.

Terrorism scares people. That's where the name comes from. But even people opposed to setting bombs or killing people will smile at gestures that make the boss look stupid. That kind of rebellion is contagious. That kind of rebellion encourages more behavior of the same kind. It's the main reason why police in totalitarian countries seem so determined to catch the unknown parties who draw big bushy moustaches on the propaganda posters of El Presidente. The big bushy moustache doesn't hurt anybody, per se. It doesn't inconvenience the government a whit. But it does undermine the government's self-importance, in the eyes of the people, which can be dangerous indeed.

With this in mind, Harry Potter is not the hero of *Order of the Phoenix*, at least insofar as the threat of Dolores Umbridge is concerned. (Or at all, considering that the attack on the Ministry turns out to be a big mistake.) He remains relatively ineffectual against her. There's a reason it feels so deeply satisfying when Fred and George drive her to fury and then blithely fly off, calling her an old bat. They're the ones who demonstrate, by vivid example, that Umbridge cannot remain in power as long as those she seeks to terrorize simply refuse to cooperate with her.

They're the heroes. They're the inspirations.

And it's a good thing they're around to strike the blow.

Because, as a sad Dumbledore notes at the end of the book, "'(Harry has) enough responsibility to be going on with'" (*Order of the Phoenix* 844).

Put it all together and what does it mean?

The best novels are not only about what they merely seem to be about. A great story is not just an engine to drive the readers from one page to the next. The best are fueled not just by make-believe, but by the very same issues that drive the real world the authors and readers live in. Such resonances may not be immediately obvious to those caught up in the stories. But they exist just the same, giving the narratives a weight they might not possess otherwise.

It's worth noting, then, that it's possible for some readers to identify Umbridge's behavior as not so much politically repressive as single-mindedly mean. They may even leave the book imagining Umbridge's agenda to come from Voldemort, and not the Ministry. There is nothing particularly wrong with this. Everybody absorbs a story with the experience they bring to it, and you don't need to know that L. Frank Baum was commenting on the monetary gold standard, a major controversy of his time, to appreciate the comical self-delusion of the denizens of Emerald City in *The Wizard of Oz*.

The fact is, Umbridge *is* mean. She clearly takes great pleasure in her mission to break Harry's spirit, whether that includes attacking his reputation, depriving him of the after-school sport that gives him so much pleasure, or downright torturing him at every opportunity.

And she is very much an "ally" of Voldemort, if not in actual fact, then at least in type. . . .

CHAPTER TWENTY

Hogwarts:
The Curriculum

Wow, that was some heavy stuff. We'll return to our examinations of the Harry Potter cast, before long, but after six separate chapters probing people who make the poor lad's life miserable, we definitely need a palate-cleanser.

So let's turn to the curriculum at Hogwarts, and devote a few words to the classes they teach, as well as a few they don't.

It's a given that the wizarding world operates by a different set of rules, and that basic required knowledge among Muggles is not the same thing as basic required knowledge among wizards.

This goes both ways, of course. That's how we get Ron's comical ignorance of the proper way to use telephones, and his father's equally comical fascination with basic Muggle technology. Indeed, one of the great unspoken ironies of the entire series is that a great friendship could have been born, between Arthur Weasley and Vernon Dursley, had the latter not been such a nasty piece of work. Think of it. Eliminate Dursley's bigotry toward wizards, and render him a nice guy who can tolerate, if not precisely understand, the world inhabited by his strange nephew, and all of a sudden he becomes one of Arthur's favorite people, willing to spend hours and hours and hours telling the fascinated wizard everything he knows about drills. Arthur would see Vernon as an endless source of entertaining information. Vernon would see Arthur as a rather down-to-earth fellow who shares his one all-consuming passion. It's almost too bad that the two must remain at odds. In a different world, they'd be life-long friends.

Still, one of the cuter things about Hogwarts is the way some of its subjects parallel those you'd find in Muggle schools, with but a change in emphasis and affect.

For instance, what is Potions, but the wizarding equivalent of chemistry? It's still a matter of mixing all the correct ingredients in the correct proportions, and knowing what to expect as they interact. The forces at play are different, as are the theories the students need to learn in order to understand why they should expect one effect instead of another, but the physical processes are similar. We're willing to bet that the same can be said of the smells. And what is Herbology but the wizarding equivalent of botany? What is Arithmency but a discipline related to Muggle mathematics?

History of Magic is, of course, easy to compare to our Muggle equivalent, up to and including the wide gap between its fascinating potential and the way it's all too often ruined by droning teachers who turn the whole thing into a deadly dull, colorless exercise in the memorization of dates. Your Friendly Host was fortunate enough, in his own school days, to learn history from some teachers who brought passion and enthusiasm to the events they covered, making those old days come alive instead of sealing them in the endless fly-in-amber dullness Harry and friends suffer at the undead hands of Professor Binns. But he had the other kind, too, and he knows why so many Muggle kids consider their history boring.

It's worth asking, by the way: Why, exactly, did Rowling make Binns such a dullard, especially when a firm knowledge of the history of Magic would have proved immensely helpful when it came to dealing with such issues as the persecution of Giants and conflict between wizards and centaurs? Not to mention more recent subjects like the crimes of You-Know-Who? The answer is, you should only excuse the phrase,

Dead Simple. It's a writer's shortcut. Rowling wanted to create a rich and detailed fantasy world with a rich and detailed history, but she couldn't have wanted to waste precious effort and even-more-precious pages telling us all about the many centuries of wizards that lived and died and fought their various wars before Harry ever came on the scene. She had a story to get on with. So she cheated, if you want to call it that, and created a teacher who could cover all of that without ever engaging Harry's full attention. It's enough for a dazed Harry to stagger out of that impossibly dull class, with vague and confused impressions of endless detail about disputes and wars and trade agreements and the like . . . an arrangement that establishes the existence of that much detail without forcing readers to slog through any of it ourselves.

Harry gets all the glory. He might as well handle all the heavy lifting and listen to all of that stuff, so we don't have to. If there's anything we truly need to know, as the story progresses, he can be reminded or told for the first time by Dumbledore, or Hagrid, or know-it-all Hermione, instead of leaving us suffering, as Harry must suffer, at the hands of Professor Binns.

The presence of Astronomy, as opposed to Astrology, is interesting. You would normally expect Astrology, a medieval belief-system tying the stars to events on Earth, to play a larger role at a school devoted to Magic. It's absolute bunk, of course, and dangerous bunk at that—please don't send your Friendly Host outraged letters, because it is—but then, this is a fantasy universe involving Magic and Prophecies and Mythical Creatures and other things. Astrology would seem to belong there. Instead, it only appears in the teachings of Professor Trelawney, who is most of the time a pathetic fraud who deludes herself as much as she wastes the time of her students. Later we get a few choice words from the centaur Firenze, who with his very presence establishes himself as one of the Hogwarts teachers we're intended to trust as a true authority on his subject. He calls Astrology "'human nonsense,'" and explains that "'tiny human accidents . . . are of no more significance than the scurryings of ants to the wide universe, and are unaffected by planetary movements'" (*Order of the Phoenix* 603).

You couldn't be clearer than that. Your Friendly Host can only wonder why Rowling is so adamant on the subject. Maybe it comes from her deep awareness that these stories are being read by children, who could use the reality check. Maybe she's encountered one too many reader with a less than solid grasp on the difference between magic she made up to tell a story and magic as an actual belief system. Or maybe she wanted to establish Firenze as an expert far more reliable than Trelawney is most of the time. Either way, it's there. And not even the late Carl Sagan, a very smart astronomer and opponent of Astrology whose wonderful books you should seek out and read if you haven't done so already, could have put it better.

(One can only wonder if the centaur's lesson about the true nature of the universe qualifies as, please don't throw this book across the room, Firenzic Science.)

In Astrology's place, Hogwarts teaches what seems to be true Astronomy, a science that maps the heavens in the context of a fact-based curriculum that both probes the structure of the universe and explores the birth of all matter in the celestial cauldron of the stars. At Hogwarts it isn't connected to any related Muggle disciplines, such as physics, but rather stands by itself, perhaps as a necessary reminder that both magical and non-magical creatures stand under the same sky. It's an interesting inclusion.

It's not nearly as thought-provoking, however, as the host of Muggle subjects Hogwarts does not seem to cover at all, not even as wizarding equivalents. Let's take a look at those.

The most obvious omission is English Composition. Why is that a problem? Well, think about the kind of kind of homework Hogwarts students have to do, day in and day out. They have to write a two-foot scroll on Potions, a six-inch scroll on Charms, another foot-long scroll on some obscure event from the fifteenth century, and so on. That's an awful lot of writing. Granted that all of these kids learned how to read and write the traditional way, before any of them ever boarded the Hogwarts Express, are they all accomplished wordsmiths by age ten? Aren't there any who need more help organizing their thoughts in some coherent manner? Or are there some who hand in homework that looks like this:

Bernard Bumbly
Hufflepuff
Third-Year Poshuns
Proffesr Snape's Class
Heeling poshuns are verry important. If you dont mix your hee
Heeling poshun the rite way you cood be in serius truble so to mix a
Heeling poshun that WORKS fill the vessel with water then put in
too pinches of Gumble weed fallowed by a hanful of dragon scales
which you MUST MIX 1ˢᵗ but only after make sure that the
Gumble weed is dry if its not dry it will turn to purrpil smoke and
any body that breathes it in will find out that there nose has turned
into a spoon & the only way to fix a nose that has terned into a
spoon is to. line the Bottom with froglivvers.

We take a brief and delighted pause here to imagine that wonderful twitch in Severus Snape's left eye, when he finds this essay, or something like it, among the works he needs to grade that night. But that leads to the question. Assuming that poor Bernard's grasp of "Poshuns" is indeed accurate, if poorly organized and horribly expressed, will Severus Snape take points off his passing grade? Will he suggest, in his usual sneer, that Bernard spend some time boning up on the other kind of spelling that all good wizards need? Or will he have no recourse but to ignore Bernard's composition problems entirely, on the grounds that Hogwarts offers no remedial courses on this all-important subject?

Related to that is the seeming complete absence of any courses in literature. We know that Hogwarts has an extensive library, and Diagon Alley does include at least one teeming bookstore. But unless you count the memoirs of Gilderoy Lockhart, and the questionable journalism to be found in various wizarding newspapers, there doesn't seem to be much in the way of fiction. Can this be so? Doesn't the wizarding world have its own canon of great stories, written by great authors who explore immortal themes in sagas filled with keen insight into the wizarding condition? Must a witch or wizard desperate for some escapist reading make do with books scavenged from Muggle shelves, books filled with odd characters and odder controversies that have nothing whatsoever to say to those raised according to the precepts of a wizarding lifestyle?

Similarly, there don't seem to be any art classes, given the gallery of portraits that line every wall in every important wizarding home or building. Granted that witches and wizards may not produce art the same way that we do—for all we know, they simply wave their wands at the canvas and shout, "*Cubista!*" or "*Impressionisto!*" to capture portraits that not only look like their subjects but also move and speak like them—all of this has to come from somewhere. And, as with the loss of literature, the wizarding world turns into a rather shallow one, without the perspective art brings. All of this is being learned somewhere, but not at Hogwarts, which, without it, seems to become a trade school of sorts, filled with practical knowledge but very little to nourish the actual soul. And a well-rounded education does need food for the soul, because most of us don't have pieces of ours distributed for safekeeping in Horcruxes, stashed away in places like underground lakes filled to the brim with zombies.

Ditto with music classes. We know the wizarding world has music. We've seen the instruments. We've even seen bands. Where are young wizards learning to play? Where are they finding out about the various great composers of the past? Is everybody just plinking store-bought guitars until they manage to pick up a chord or three?

Heck, what about Home Economics? Not everybody has a platoon of oppressed house-elves, doing all their cooking and cleaning for them. Some have to make do for themselves. Do you honestly believe that there's no skill involved in what Molly Weasley does? Or that she's only a member of the Order of the Phoenix because Dumbledore needs somebody to put up the coffee? When Harry enters his bachelor days (assuming he enters his bachelor days), is he going to eat out every night, or just pig out on all the junk food he snags from the candy shop at Hogsmeade? If so, will we finally see actual participation in the story from Hermione's parents, the Dentists?

How about Foreign Languages?

Now, this is a major one. *Goblet of Fire* establishes, for the benefit of those of us who imagined otherwise, that the wizarding world extends far beyond Great Britain. There are other schools in other lands, all of whom communicate in languages other than English. As far as we get to see, in the books, this manifests in the form of exotic accents. We can assume for the sake of argument that witches and wizards dealing with others of their kind, in distant lands, exercise some kind of translation spell. But we also know that the language barrier is a very real one when it comes with dealing with various non-human creatures. So let's ask. If wizards don't need to learn, for instance, Arabic or Mandarin or Urdu, do any of them need to study hard to learn Merpeople?

Or are they the equivalent of the people targeted by this joke:

What do you call somebody who speaks three languages?
Trilingual.

What you call somebody who speaks two languages?
Bilingual.

And somebody who speaks only one language?
American.

Would it be equally appropriate to substitute the word "wizard," in that punchline? That is, as long as that wizard doesn't speak Parseltongue, which is an inherited gift and not a learned one? Clearly not. But who's learning those foreign languages? Does it require work, or can it be done with a flourish of a magic wand?

But all of that can be fudged away as just missing detail.

You want to know the one class missing at Hogwarts?

Your Friendly Host, who was an unathletic kid and remains an unathletic adult, is rather abashed to be noting this.

But he finds that he must.

What about Physical Education?

What about . . . Gym?

Don't talk to me about Quidditch. That's a team sport. Many try out, but only a few are chosen. Fine, so those few get regular exercise.

What about everybody else?

Well, everybody gets flying lessons. That requires at least some degree of muscular control.

But so does riding a motorbike. We can't see that flying a broom takes care of all the body's physical needs.

Your Friendly Host is deadly serious about this.

What is the wizarding world? A place where people perform spells by means of waving their wands in highly specific flourishes.

The books have provided us with any number of cases where a student made the wrong gesture and as a result caused an entirely inappropriate effect.

Wouldn't the ability to whip out and properly wield a wand suffer from stiffness? From insufficient coordination? From weakness? From fat?

Every time Cletus tried to turn the cat into a salt shaker, his lack of muscular development interfered. "I have got to lay off the Bernie Bott beans," he fretted.

Heck, forget that.

Let's talk about magical duels. Defense of the Dark Arts includes basic dueling technique. We know from the battles fought for keeps that the skills required to survive in any duel against an experienced and determined enemy include among them the ability to dive for cover, or failing that to run like hell. How are any Hogwarts students going to survive such trials if they get winded from climbing a flight of stairs?

Let's go even further than that.

Let's talk about the Grand Event, the Triwizard Tournament.

This one contest, during the one year we get to witness it, includes a close encounter with a dragon, a long-distance underwater swim, and a race through a treacherous hedge maze. Accept the required magical skills as a given, handing them out for free at the start of the race, and you're still left with a contest that requires its students to be at the very peak of physical condition. Harry Potter, the kid who fought the troll in his first year and the Basilisk in his second, barely makes it out alive. Why would Dumbledore, or anybody, expect any Hogwarts student who hasn't enrolled in a compulsory program of extensive physical training to make it through any of these events intact, let alone the victor?

"Magic" is not a sufficient answer.

We also know that when Harry shows up at school, Dumbledore considers him skinny and underfed (a footprint of his time with the Dursleys).

Before long he's a physical paragon, not only the star athlete at the school's number one sport, but the hero who can outrun and outdodge monsters while simultaneously out-thinking the various incarnations of Lord Voldemort.

This does not just pop out of nowhere.

Somewhere, he picked up some physical conditioning.

So does Neville, the clumsy fat kid who may retain that physical type (in the books, at least—a genuine physical transformation having overtaken young Matthew Lewis, who plays the role in the movies), but proves more than capable of carrying his end of a fight, in *Order of the Phoenix*.

How does he get that, except by narrative magic, unless he's doing something with his school years other than just hitting the books?

We could try to explain this away by saying, "Well, yes, Hogwarts does have an extensive Physical Education program. It's compulsory for all students. Rowling just doesn't show it, that's all, because nothing important to the story ever actually happens there."

That would be fair enough.

Except that we know it's not true.

Rowling is very scrupulous about informing us of Harry's entire course load. When the academics get rough, she shows us quite vividly that Harry and company have trouble getting everything done with the limited number of hours in every day.

There's no room in her narrative for a hidden gym class that she just happens to avoid mentioning. There just isn't.

Nor is there room for classes covering any of the other neglected subjects discussed here. The kids who can't run, the kids who can't compose a coherent sentence, and the kids who can't find help realizing artistic ambitions, receive no help at Hogwarts. No help at all.

But turning teacups into hamsters?

That, they graduate knowing how to do. . . .

CHAPTER TWENTY-ONE

Neville the Wild Card

I n some parallel universe, just a couple of inches removed from our own, the entire story is about him.

He's the one Voldemort fails to kill, the one who receives that distinctive scar on his forehead, the one who becomes known as the Boy Who Lived, and the one who becomes the target of all those urban legends and assassination attempts.

Neville, not Harry.

No less an authority than Professor Dumbledore himself—and since when has he ever been wrong about anything?—believes that Trelawney's prophecy could have meant either Harry or Neville, before Voldemort cemented the proper interpretation with that famous failed assassination of baby Harry.

This is the likely case.

But is Neville still out of the running?

Your Friendly Host doesn't think so.

Because there's another law, cast in stone, which just might be powerful enough to trump a few spooky words, from dotty old Sybill.

And that's this:

Stories aren't always about the person they seem to be about.

Your Friendly Host can name any number of well-known stories about a legendary, heroic figure who comes to town to fight a great wrong. He is helped in this endeavor by a local, who believes himself unable to handle the crisis himself. Those of us reading the story, or seeing the film, know that the local is just a sidekick, who may help out a little bit, but will definitely fall out just before the action-packed climax, so the hero we recognize and root for can grab all the glory.

And then something happens.

It's the hero who proves not up to the job.

The sidekick has to step forward and become the hero himself.

Later, thinking over the story we've been told, we realize that we should have expected this. Our hero entered the story strong, confident, an icon destined from birth to take out the bad guys. We could name him, as the character worth watching, from a thousand paces.

But all along, without realizing it, we were also being fed information about this other guy. The nobody. The sidekick. We were being shown what his life was like and why this battle mattered to him and why he thought he couldn't handle the menace himself and exactly what he'd put at risk if he tried. He's the one whose destiny changes if he steps up, the one who changes in our estimation if he wins.

We're left realizing that the story was about him all along.

Stories aren't always about the person they seem to be about.

Is this what J. K. Rowling is up to?

Is this story going to turn out to be about Neville?

Let us examine, for a moment, what we know about this lad.

We know that from the first time we see him, he seems to be little more than just another comic-relief character. He's the one who keeps losing things, the one who keeps forgetting the password to get into the Gryffindor dormitory, the one who always quails in fear and the one who silly things keep happening to. Whenever J. K. Rowling needs somebody to be inadequate, or low-grade incompetent, she picks Neville.

But there are also indications that we're supposed to watch him, indications that, from the first book onward, tell his story without ever bringing him into the foreground.

We find out that he's an orphan like Harry, that he's been raised by a grandmother who seems to baby him and belittle him at every opportunity, that he's physically awkward, and that he's not a great student except at Herbology.

We learn that while he seems timid, he's more than capable of standing up to his friends.

We learn that his anger and heartbreak, at the family that has been taken from him, is just as great as Harry's. We only see it in brief glimpses, as when he tackles a thoroughly deserving Draco Malfoy, or when he's left sobbing on the stairs by the Moody imposter's demonstration of the Cruciatis Curse.

We also find out that he has a fierce kind of pride. When Harry and friends accidentally encounter Neville's shattered parents, at St. Mungo's, Neville meets their stares with a certain shamed defiance. *This is my life,* his stare seems to say. *Go ahead. Mock me for it.* Harry, Ron, and Hermione are too decent to ever dream of doing such a thing. But doesn't that do wonders for setting up Neville's heroism, at the end of *Order of the Phoenix,* when he puts himself on the line to help Harry at the Ministry of Magic?

Doesn't that leave you wondering if there isn't a little more to Neville?

Dumbledore assures Harry that the champion of Trelawney's prophecy has to have been personally marked by Voldemort. That seems to indicate Harry, all right. But isn't the same true, in a different way, of Neville? His whole life has been marked by Voldemort. He has spent his days in the shadow of the evils at Voldemort's command. Unlike Harry, he has never been famous, or a hero. He has rarely even been seen as adequate. But we already know that he's more than he seems to be. We know he's wounded, but determined.

The story certainly *seems* to be about Harry.

Just look at the titles on those book jackets.

But what is a story, but something that matters in the life of the person living it?

What is a story, but something that changes the person at its center?

Who does any of this matter to, more than Neville?

And who has grown more, and changed more, than Neville?

Or to put it another way: Has your opinion of Harry changed, all that much, since *Sorcerer's Stone?*

Probably not.

He's pretty much the same kid he always was. Only smarter and more grown up and more determined.

What about your opinion of Neville?

Well, um. Gee.

There is an entire checklist of Unresolved Questions that J. K. Rowling will likely need to resolve, in *Deathly Hallows*. Wait a few pages and we'll provide it. But Neville is one of the major ones. The novel itself will prove whether we're at right on this one, but at this point it seems impossible to believe that the action will not come back to Hogwarts at some point, and that Neville will not play some kind of significant role. Certainly we can expect some kind of confrontation between him and Bellatrix Lestrange. If anybody other than Neville takes care of her, we'll be seriously disappointed.

But is it possible that he'll be the one who takes care of Voldemort, as well? This, we don't know.

Your Friendly Host strongly suspects that this role will fall to Harry, after all. Harry is the kid whose name appears on the cover on every book, the one who will be best remembered by those more casual readers who tend to forget plot details between one volume and the next. Many of those will have trouble remembering that Harry has a friend named Neville at all. And if you think that a stretch, please be apprised that Your Friendly Host knows somebody with a Swiss cheese memory who has read all the books and seen all the movies and still has trouble remembering that all of the menaces our Harry encounters are connected by the shadow of one big villain named Lord Voldemort. This friend honestly needed help figuring out who that snaky-looking guy at the end of the *Goblet of Fire* movie was. Tell this friend that the big story is not about Harry at all, but instead that kid who gets lifted up by his ears in *Chamber of Secrets*, and he'll just say, "Who!?!?" Your Friendly Host suspects that many of J. K. Rowling's younger readers, who are not yet up to the task of following nuances, will react to any revelation painting Neville as Number One Hero with equal puzzlement and confusion.

But again, it's *Deathly Hallows* which will reveal the truth.

And the only thing we can ultimately say about Neville's role in the climax is that, if we're wrong and the story does turn out to have been about him all along . . . that J. K. Rowling has played fair with us.

She's laid the foundations.

Divers Others

Then there are the rest of them, the characters who live and breathe but exist around the periphery of the action. We may not know enough about them to merit extended discussion not already covered in previous pages, but they do prompt a comment or two. In no particular order:

Moaning Myrtle
Didn't this poor girl have any friends or relatives who might be upset to learn that she's damned to spend eternity as a disembodied spirit in a Hogwarts bathroom? I mean, at least The Bloody Baron and Nearly Headless Nick have been there for centuries. It's pretty much a given that their social circle has all died out by now. But people knew Myrtle. Even if she was as insufferable as a living, breathing girl as she is as a ghost, which seems likely, isn't there one acquaintance, anywhere, concerned

161

by her legendary status as the specter who never stops whining? Isn't there anybody who would visit her, try to comfort her, offer inducements that would prompt her to move on?

Filch

The caretaker who always wants to whip the kids, and never gets to, always complains about the messes he's left having to pick up. You might think he's just an irritable old pud until you consider that he's *the* caretaker, and Hogwarts seems to be the size of several Pentagons, even without its network of hidden rooms and secret passages. Granted that his labors are supported at least in part by Hogwarts huge complement of house-elves, how on earth does he ever catch up with his mopping?

Fleur

The impossibly beautiful French girl who dazzles Ron, affiances Bill, and deeply annoys Molly Weasley is evidence of more than the pressing need of a hidden foreign-language program. She also provides one of the series's greatest romantic moments when she angrily proclaims her love for Bill after the damage done to his face in the climax of *Half-Blood Prince*. At that moment, Mrs. Weasley realizes that she has greatly underestimated the woman her son is determined to marry. There are no great mysteries here, just the acknowledgment of a splendid character payoff owned by someone whose business might have been over and done with after her participation in the Triwizard Tournament during *Goblet of Fire*. (We don't know if her defiant declaration of love will make the movie version of *Half-Blood Prince*. But it damned well better.)

Fred and George Weasley

Two more characters whose greatest achievement came with their departure from Hogwarts, following their prank sabotage of Dolores Umbridge in *Order of the Phoenix*. They earned cheers with that moment. One wonders if any key moment in Harry's ultimate showdown with Lord Voldemort will come down to the magical equivalent of a whoopee cushion, purchased from their establishment.

Percy Weasley

We devoted significant acreage, in the "Ron" chapters, to the precise connotation of the surname "Weasley." We evoke that thought again, now, that the specific combination of "Percy" and "Weasley" implies a character exactly like this one turns out to be. Remarkable for being the only member of that large clan to grow up as a huge prat focused on his career to the extent of all considerations, he emerges as proof that you cannot always choose your family and that if we could we might in some ways be better off. Chances are he will see the error of his ways by the end of *Deathly Hallows*. Absent any genuine heroics, Your Friendly Host votes to continue considering him a prat.

Peter Pettigrew ("Scabbers," "Wormtail")

The vilest of all traitors, the man so pathetic that he gave up his humanity for years to hide in the form of a pet rat, has been outed by (the real-life) *Wizard* magazine, among others, as the one character, aside from Voldemort himself, most responsible for the evils that bedevil our characters in the course of the series. He betrayed Harry's parents, helped frame Sirius, cared for the incapacitated Voldemort, and brought Voldemort back to life. He deserves one heck of an end, and one of the pleasures of *Deathly Hallows* will be seeing him get one. And yet, notice one thing: Unlike many villains, he never really gets rewarded for his crimes, does he? He just buys himself fleeting moments of safety, or comfort, in the shadow of beings more powerful than himself. People sometimes talk about the banality of evil. He is living evidence that unless you're the boss, evil sometimes sells its services at rock-bottom prices.

Luna Lovegood

The odd, spacy crackpot among Harry's circle may be an object of low comedy, but who can break our hearts more, with a few offhanded words revealing her perception of herself as despised and friendless? And who is easier to love, with her splendid off-target theories and spooky candor? Bless J. K. Rowling for not making us wait forever to see her, in *Order of the Phoenix*, show her mettle as a hero. Bless her for giving Harry his only real comfort, following the apparent death of Sirius. Bless Harry for defiantly identifying her, at the start of *Half-Blood Prince*, as a friend. And Bless Ron, whose stunned realization of his affection for her, also in *Half-Blood Prince*, mirrors that of Your Friendly Host. But we do have one question: Why, exactly, are her pronouncements about "gulping plimpies" and the like any more crazy than what Hogwarts students are expected to believe on a daily basis?

Petunia Dursley
One of the biggest surprises of the Harry Potter books is the revelation that she's heard of Dementors and may indeed be more clued in about the wizarding world than she lets on. Nothing will, of course, excuse her treatment of Harry (since even her influence would have softened the excessive emotional abuse practiced by her husband Vernon). J. K. Rowling has hinted that there's more to her than we've seen. If so, we'll find out during Harry's last visit to his reprehensible Uncle and Aunt, in *Deathly Hallows*.

Dudley Dursley
Harry's bullying cousin doesn't have to be on stage for many pages before he establishes that he embodies everything J. K. Rowling would like her young readers to avoid becoming. He's stupid, not in the manner of people who don't have a choice but in the manner of those who choose that quality for themselves, as a lifestyle choice. He is greedy, spoiled, destructive, piggish, a thug both in manners and in practice—in all ways a child who might not have been as special as Harry, but did not have to be as damaged as his mother and father have made him. One of the odder things about the Harry Potter novels is that this thoroughly awful child grows to be a thoroughly awful teen, and is yet easy to see as a figure of pity, by the later volumes. Unlike Harry, he has nothing to look forward to. He will always be what he is now. It is doubtful that Rowling imagines any greater fate for him.

The Marauders (James, Sirius, Remus, and Peter)
The four musketeers of a past generation of Hogwarts may be remembered with fondness, by anybody who wasn't personally touched by the casual cruelty James was known for showing outsiders like the young Severus Snape, but cracks have appeared in that historical façade. We now know that James was not always the paragon he is remembered as being, that their reputation for breaking the rules sometimes came at the cost of real hurt done to real people, that even as an adult Sirius was still capable of admiring recklessness for its own sake, and that the minor evils of their time together may have had repercussions that continue to Harry's present day. Their shared past as Animagus shape-changers, began as a gesture of solidarity for Lupin's werewolf activities, makes them literally what they were, at the time: wild things. In context, the

incantation that unlocks the staggeringly helpful Marauder's Map, ("I solemnly swear that I am up to no good,") that at first seems a harmless, tongue-in-cheek ode to teenage mischief, now takes on a more ominous tone, given our current doubts about just how dark their activities became. It's hard to believe that any of these people, Pettigrew aside, ever engaged in any evil deeper than unthinking, unexamined bullying, but we have reason to doubt, and to fear what we might find out in that upcoming final volume.

CHAPTER TWENTY-THREE

The Most Satisfying Moments in the Harry Potter Series (So Far)

And then come the moments that defy analysis, the ones that may not provide grist for endless discussion but which resonate because they make us jump up and down in our seats.

This list is Your Friendly Host indulging himself. You might well come up with an entirely different one. You will, for instance, find only one Quidditch victory on this list; if those are your favorite chapters, you are about to be sorely disappointed. You will also notice a substantial bias on behalf of *Order of the Phoenix* and *Half-Blood Prince*, that that may just be because the first is the darkest of the Harry Potter to date and is accordingly all the most satisfying during its moments of relative light, and the second pays off storylines that began in prior volumes. (Or you could just say that your Host likes them best, which is just as accurate.) We have therefore provided several blank lines in case you feel the need to add to his compendium.

1. *Sorcerer's Stone*, pages 46–60: Harry's cruel childhood at the hands of the unloving Dursleys is interrupted by the arrival of Hagrid, who informs him he's a wizard, brings him his first birthday cake, tells off Uncle Vernon and Aunt Petunia, and gives Dudley a pig's tail, for good measure.

2. *Sorcerer's Stone*, pages 178–179: Following the adventure of the mountain troll, Hermione becomes the third friend in the trio.

3. *Sorcerer's Stone*, pages 288–309: Harry defeats Quirrell/Voldemort, and ends his first year in school.

4. *Chamber of Secrets*, page 303: Gilderoy Lockhart gets a taste of his own medicine.

5. *Chamber of Secrets*, page 322: Harry defeats Tom Riddle.

6. *Chamber of Secrets*, pages 337–339: Harry brilliantly tricks Lucius Malfoy into freeing his abused house-elf, Dobby.

7. *Prisoner of Azkaban*, pages 22–30: We meet, instantly despise, and say a happy goodbye to Marge Dursley, who gets exactly what's coming to her.

8. *Prisoner of Azkaban*, pages 136–137: The much put-upon Neville defeats the Boggart taking the form of Professor Snape.

9. *Prisoner of Azkaban*, pages 378–435: A revelation-packed climax that includes the unmasking of Scabbers; Harry's discovery that Sirius Black is innocent and that he, therefore, has a family that loves him; Hermione's unveiling of the Time-Turner; Harry's successful summoning of a Patronus; the concurrent demonstration that he really does have a lot in common with his dad; and the rescues of Buckbeak and Sirius Black.

10. *Goblet of Fire*, pages 352–356: Harry prevails in the first task of the Triwizard Tournament.

11. *Goblet of Fire*, page 358: After a stony silence that has separated the two friends for weeks, "Harry knew Ron was about to apologize and suddenly he found he didn't need to hear it." Exactly right.

12. *Goblet of Fire*, pages 727–728: Hermione serenely reveals the horrible revenge she's taken on Rita Skeeter.

13. *Order of the Phoenix*, page 90: Sirius reminds Molly Weasley that Harry's not her son. She fiercely replies, "He's as good as!" It's her best moment.

14. *Order of the Phoenix*, pages 325–327: Hermione brings up the idea of Harry teaching forbidden Defense Against the Dark Arts classes. He has no idea what she's talking about. Ron calls him stupid for not getting it. A vital moment in Harry's evolution as hero.

15. *Order of the Phoenix*, pages 612–623: The exposure of "Dumbledore's Army" hits the great wizard where he lives. Dumbledore covers for Harry and refuses to submit to arrest under Cornelius Fudge's orders.

16. *Order of the Phoenix*, pages 661–665: During a career conference, Professor McGonagall angrily stands up to Dolores Umbridge on Harry's behalf.

17. *Order of the Phoenix*, pages 673–675: Fred and George Weasley humiliate Dolores Umbridge, and fly off to start their practical-joke shop, after announcing to an awestruck student body: "Special discounts to Hogwarts students who swear they're going to use our products to get rid of this old bat!"

18. *Order of the Phoenix*, pages 701–702: Returning to the Quidditch stadium after a dispiriting rendezvous with Hagrid, Harry and Hermione suddenly realize they hear Gryffindor students singing "Weasley is our king!"

19. *Order of the Phoenix*, page 761: Ginny, Neville, and Luna all stand up to Harry, declaring their right as members of Dumbledore's Army to fly to the Ministry alongside him.

20. *Order of the Phoenix*, pages 868–870: Arthur Weasley, Nymphadora Tonks, Mad-Eye Moody, and Lupin all confront Vernon Dursley at the railway station, assuring him that if Harry is mistreated again, they will hear about it.

21. *Half-Blood Prince*, pages 45–56: Dumbledore visits Harry at the Dursley home and slowly builds from politeness to righteous anger. "You did not do as I asked. You did not treat Harry as a son. He has known nothing, but neglect and often cruelty at your hands. The best that can be said is that he has at least escaped the appalling damage you have inflicted on the unfortunate boy sitting between you." Wonderful, and like Harry's forgiveness of Ron in *Goblet of Fire*, precisely right.

22. *Half-Blood Prince*, pages 293–300: Gryffindor Quidditch captain bolsters lagging teammate Ron with a magical placebo.

23. *Half-Blood Prince*, pages 341–348. Rufus Scrimgeour attempts to draft Harry as propaganda tool of the Ministry. Harry will have none of it. It's a great scene, line by line, but it ends with that perfect punchline, Scrimgeour sneering, "Dumbledore's man, through and through, aren't you, Potter," and Harry replying, "Yeah, I am."

24. *Half-Blood Prince*, pages 357–358: Dumbledore's composure wavers just a tad when this conversation is reported to him. The old softie.

25. *Half-Blood Prince*, pages 533–534: Harry and Ginny kiss for the first time.

26. *Half-Blood Prince*, pages 622–624: Fleur, who is not Molly Weasley's ideal of a prospective daughter-in-law, defiantly announces her intent to stay by her wounded Bill's side. "You thought I would not weesh to marry him? Or, per'aps, hoped? . . . What do I care how he looks, I am good-looking enough for both of us, I theenk!" How many ways can we put it? Precisely right.

27. *Half-Blood Prince*, pages 633–652: Following Dumbledore's funeral, Harry defies Scrimgeour a second time, and announces his intention to go after Voldemort himself. Ron and Hermione insist on joining him. I don't know about you, but I think Voldemort's in trouble.

Space reserved for *Deathly Hallows* highlights:

28. _____

_____

29. _____

_____

30. _____

_____

31. _____

_____

32. _____

_____

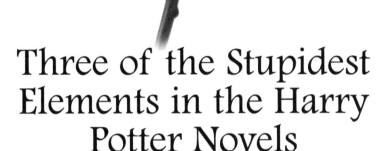

CHAPTER TWENTY-FOUR

Three of the Stupidest Elements in the Harry Potter Novels

E ven the best fiction writers make missteps. William Shakespeare's *Hamlet* is predicated on the idea that a prince banished from his ancestral home because of a murder committed in the heat of passion can return, in the next act, not much later in real time, with nobody but the son of the dead man still carrying a grudge for that crime.

Daniel Defoe's *Robinson Crusoe* contains a scene where a man strips himself naked, swims out to a shipwreck, and fills his pockets with scavenged goods. William Golding's *Lord of the Flies* entirely depends on a pair of spectacles the boys use to focus the sun's rays whenever they need to start fires—a fine trick, given that the specific prescription used by the boy they belong to cannot be used to focus light in this manner.

J. K. Rowling's work is not immune from such stumbles. She is capable of covering them, but they can be spotted with a little searching. We have already covered a number of the weaker points in her narrative, such as the wizarding world's incomprehensible desire to keep itself a secret from the Muggle world, in prior pages, but we're not done. There are others. Here they are:

1. *Immortality and Nicholas Flamel*
Dumbledore's partner, Nicholas Flamel, is well-known for his longevity, derived from an Immortality Elixir he creates in part by use of the Sorcerer's Stone. The Stone is destroyed at the end of the book of the same name, raising the important question of why Voldemort, whose entire gig is making himself indestructible, had in previous years gone to such extreme lengths protecting himself with Horcruxes and so on. If an Immortality Elixir was available why didn't he just go after that? Or get the secret and mix up some of is own?

2. *Voldemort's Entire Plan in* Goblet of Fire
Let's review this. You're a Dark Lord. Your entire plan depends on getting your hands on a certain young boy, who is currently attending the school run by the *One Wizard You Fear*. To get your hands on this boy, all you have to do is get him to touch a Port Key capable of transporting him to your location. Because of safeguards already in place you cannot do this unless he is outside the school. Rather than arrange for one of your many minions to give the boy a valuable gift, which can be activated after he leaves school, or to lure him to another location such as the Forbidden Forest, which is also not at all difficult given that this particular boy has a long history of not staying put when told, you arrange for this boy's highly suspicious enlistment in a competition capable of killing him. You do this even though it immediately raises suspicions that something fishy must be up. You do this even though you have already managed to replace one of the boy's teachers that year, a trusted authority figure with an impeccable pedigree, with an imposter, who as a teacher can simply overpower the kid or otherwise order him to come along on an "important errand," no questions asked. You do this even though the competition in question has a long history of causing fatalities, and that this kid is a couple of years too young to possess all the knowledge he needs to prevail, without significant help. You do this even though the last thing you want is for the kid to die before he can restore you to health, as his premature death will leave you weak and

174

shrunken and looking like a hobbit larvae. You do this even though the entire competition is being watched by the *One Wizard You Fear*, who will have months and months and months to suss out exactly what you have planned, and is most likely to suspect your plot of coming to head at the last moment it possibly can. Finally, you put your Port Key at the end of a treacherous hedge maze, which can quite easily kill him before he comes close to being able to touch it—or where it can be found, first, by any one of three other competitors likely to get there before him, thus leaving you exactly where you started before you went to all this time and trouble. Let's face it, Mr. Dark Lord. As evil plots go, this one is filled with more holes than Albert Hall. It only succeeds at all because the *One Wizard You Fear*, throughout this entire chain of events, so blind that he qualifies as more stupid than you must have been, to rest all your hopes of resurrection on this cockamamie plan.

3. *Time-Turners*

This device capable of turning back the clock, which is excellent at demonstrating Hermione's driven nature, and is instrumental at enabling the action climax of *Prisoner of Azkaban*, is never once recognized as what it really is: An ultimate weapon. Armed with this device, any witch or wizard can go back in time and rearrange any circumstance to his or her own advantage. Armed with this device, any witch or wizard can prove invincible. In *Mapping The World Of Harry Potter*, edited by Mercedes Lackey, a previous volume from this publisher, Richard Garfinkle's essay "Why Killing Harry Potter Is the Worst Outcome for Voldemort" demonstrates that, armed with the Time-Turner, Hermione Granger is so much more powerful than Harry Potter or Voldemort or Dumbledore or any other wizard that she presents by far the greatest threat to the Dark Lord's murderous ambitions. She'd just react to Harry's death by going back in time, and erasing every single step of the Dark Lord's climb to power. She'd eliminate him from history. She'd bring Harry back to life and destroy the Death Eaters from within. She'd be like a pilot armed with a nuclear payload, up against an angry native armed with a spear.

Now, J. K. Rowling goes to considerable lengths to protect the sanctity of her story. Early in *Half-Blood Prince*, she confirms that the battle at the end of *Order of the Phoenix* completely destroyed the Ministry's entire supply of Time-Sorters. This is known in the trade as an author's convenience. It is the equivalent of that scene, early in any number of other books, where the hero loses the cell phone he would otherwise use to call for help. Or drops the last of his ammunition down a sewer grate, and thus establishes that he cannot get out the darkened warehouse by simply out-shooting the villain out to kill him. Your Friendly Host thinks the best example comes from a Superman story of many years ago, where the Man of Steel got out of one tough situation by using a power that rendered him even more invincible than he normally is, and thought, "Unfortunately, I can only use this power *once*! If I'm ever in this situation again, I'll have to think of *another* way out!"

Rowling destroys the Time-Turners to make sure that Hermione cannot turn back the clock and simply save Dumbledore, at the end of *Half-Blood Prince*. This measure also makes sure that whatever Harry, Ron, and Hermione do during *Deathly Hallows* reeks of permanence, and cannot be undone the first time the kids decide that any of their adventures could have been handled better. The move therefore turns a weakness into a considerable strength. But that leads to a serious question. If the Time-Turners *existed*, in quantity, and were so easy to get at that Hogwarts teachers were able to arrange for their use by dedicated students who wanted to handle more than their usual courseload, then why weren't Aurors armed with them, back in the days when Voldemort and the Death Eaters were running around killing people?

In short, Time-Turners render inevitable this scene, which would have destroyed everything:

> *The evil Lord Voldemort cast his evil gaze on the most loyal of his Death Eaters. "The time has come," he intoned sepulchrally. "You may now go forth and commence killing our enemies, including the Longbottoms and the Potters!" Lestrange and Malfoy and Goyle and the rest all bowed before their master and turned to leave. But they found the door blocked by a squad of Aurors led by the terrifying figure of Mad-Eye Moody. "You should know better than that," said Moody, his Eye darting from one face to another. "The second we found the bodies we knew that you had to be making your move at last. So we used our Time-Turners to step back a day or two and get you before you could all hop on your brooms. By the way, you're under arrest."*

Voldemort said, "B-but . . . b-but . . . b-but . . ." Oh, shut up, said Moody. Later, Dumbledore said, "It's a good thing I thought of unlocking that cabinet with all the Time-Turners. We usually give them to deserving students who need a few extra hours in the day to get through all their courses, but they're even more useful in matters of law-enforcement. Just think, if we hadn't done this, that guy might have caused some genuine inconvenience." Young Harry Potter let out a yawn in his mother's arms, and went on to live a wholly unremarkable life. The End.

CHAPTER TWENTY-FIVE

J. K. Rowling:
The Verdict of Posterity

Your Friendly Host must apologize. But he's about to show his age again.

When he was a young boy, some of his favorite books were written by a man named Hugh Lofting.

A quick look at the bookstore listings is sufficient to establish that almost none of this man's books are in print today. You have to special order the few that are.

This has very little to do with their quality.

Nor does it have to do with them being forgotten.

Chances are that you do know the name of Mr. Lofting's creation. You just don't know that he was the man responsible for first putting the stories down on paper.

The character he created was Dr. Dolittle.

And if you're like most people, right now, you will say something very much like, "Oh, yes! Like those movies with Eddie Murphy! The ones about that funky, bug-eyed veterinarian who can hear animals talk! I remember funny scenes like the one about the dog begging for mercy as he's being dragged in to be spayed! Lots of stuff like that!"

Your Friendly Host sighs and says, "No, not quite like in the movies with Eddie Murphy. Not even *close* to the movies with Eddie Murphy."

The Dr. Dolittle he remembers was a mild-mannered country doctor from the small English village of Puddleby-on-the-Marsh. This doctor's ability to speak to animals came after years of research and practice—years spent carefully writing down the sounds they made and deducing from context the meanings they stood for. He lived in relative poverty, in a cluttered house packed to the rafters with an entire menagerie of animal boarders and servants. Derided by his neighbors as a nut, and at one point obliged to defend himself in court in order to avoid being imprisoned as a lunatic, he was nevertheless a dedicated man of science, who from time to time ventured forth to distant regions of the globe in order to track down obscure species and engage in a number of other highly eccentric business enterprises. His adventures, appeared in such volumes as *The Adventures of Doctor Dolittle, The Voyages of Doctor Dolittle, Doctor Dolittle's Circus, Doctor Dolittle's Zoo*, and (believe it or not, my favorite) *Doctor Dolittle's Post Office*. They were not picture books, but actual novels, and Your Friendly Host remembers them as genuinely wonderful, filled with as many memorable characters and hairs-breadth cliffhangers as the Harry Potter books. There was even a movie more-or-less faithful to their spirit, about forty years ago, starring a man named Rex Harrison. It didn't do very well at the box office and certainly didn't capture the heights of comic invention to be found in the books about the circus and zoo.

The Dr. Dolittle movies you probably know take nothing from Hugh Lofting's books but the name of the main character. They add bathroom humor, add a whole bunch of stupid jokes, and amputate any real charm.

The much better books are, as far as Your Friendly Host can tell, pretty much entirely forgotten except by the people who grew up with them.

Your Friendly Host also adored a series of books, by various authors, about Alfred Hitchcock and The Three Investigators. Alfred Hitchcock was not the hero of these books, but—if readers who already know his name will forgive the explanation—a very famous film director in real life. When not making absolutely terrific suspense movies like *Rear Window* and *North by Northwest* and *Strangers on a Train* that you should seek out and watch right away, he poked so much fun at himself, that he became as famous as the movie stars he helped to make famous. The Three Investigators were a trio of young boys, led by a brilliant kid named Jupiter Jones, with their own detective agency who liked to drop in on Mr. Hitchcock at the movie studio to report the details of their latest cases. (The phenomenon of Mr. Hitchcock actually having the time and inclination to listen to them is, all by itself, as fantastical as anything in the Harry Potter books.) These books were so popular for so long that they continued appearing long after the real Hitchcock died. After a while the name Alfred Hitchcock was no longer quite as recognizable to younger readers as it had been, and he was replaced in the books by a made-up character not quite as interesting to those of us who only started reading the books in the first place because Alfred Hitchcock appeared in them.

Chances are that you haven't seen any of these either.

Your Friendly Host also remembers a series of books about a kid named Danny Dunn, by one Jay Williams. Danny billed himself as a "scientific detective," and got involved with various adventures with titles like *Danny Dunn and the Smallifying Machine* and *Danny Dunn and the Anti-Gravity Paint*. Oh, boy, did Your Friendly Host haunt the library for more adventures from Danny! But where is he now?

And, while we're on the subject, whatever happened to Henry Reed, teenage star of such Robert McCloskey novels as *Henry Reed's Babysitting Service* and *Henry Reed's Journey*?

Or that other great Robert McCloskey creation, the other resourceful teenage boy named *Homer Price*? Whose adventures include an amazing one involving a coffee shop endangered by a donut-making machine that refuses to be turned off?

Answer: I don't know.

These are all heroes remembered by Your Friendly Host, who won't blame you one bit if you all now think he's about 1 million years old.

He more or less is, even if some of those books were already moldy library copies when he first found and read them.

But where are they now? Who remembers them?

Then we have these questions, about another pair of resourceful boys.

Who remembers *Tom Sawyer*, by Mark Twain? Or its (first) sequel, *Huckleberry Finn*?

Pretty much everybody, that's who.

And what does all of this have to say about whether J. K. Rowling and Harry Potter will be remembered, twenty years from now, let alone 100?

Ah, that's the question.

Your Friendly Host believes it a cinch that Harry Potter will always be remembered as a phenomenon. You don't sell more books in more languages than any other fiction writer ever has, in the history of mankind, only to become a footnote.

And the movies will certainly help. Long after the films become perennials, always available on the *All Harry Potter, All the Time Network*, parents will be using the movies to occupy children on long car trips.

But will the books still be read?

Will we ever reach a point similar to the one Your Friendly Host reached in the last couple of pages, where any adults who mention the books as favorites they remember from their childhoods, risk revealing that they're grew up when there were still dinosaurs roaming the earth?

There's really no way of telling for sure.

It depends a great deal on who's coming next.

But this is what Your Friendly Host believes.

Somewhere on this planet of ours there's an aspiring author of children's books, putting off collection agencies and clipping coupons to fill the barren cupboard, whose creation is just dying to set the world on fire. Maybe it has something to do with wizards and maybe it has something to do with pirates and maybe it has something to do with outer space. We don't know. But sooner or later the books will come out and a few adventurous people will be the first to read them, and the word will spread from person to person, and the books will make the bestseller lists, and before long the person's face will start appearing on the cover of magazines, and producers will start talking about who to get for the inevitable movie versions, and all the headlines will say something like, JO SHMO: THE NEXT J. K. ROWLING?

And Jo Shmo, if she has any class at all, will say, "No, I'm not the next J. K. Rowling. And my hero is not the next Harry Potter. We already have a J. K. Rowling, and we already have a Harry Potter. God Bless them both. But there's still room for the next thing."

She will be right about that.

There will always be room for the next thing.

The question is just how many of the old things will have to be put away to make this room. How many Danny Dunns, Henry Reeds, and Dr. Dolittles will fade away and disappear because there's no longer enough space to accommodate them all.

Your Friendly Host believes that Jo Shmo's hero will be tremendously successful and tremendously popular and will spawn his own movies and his own toy line and will eventually sink back into the nothingness he came from.

This will happen, again and again, throughout the next fifty years. Maybe through the next hundred.

In many cases, this will be a shame. Some of those books will be awfully good.

But time will continue to pass.

And there will come a day when even the youngest of Harry Potter's current fans are grandparents, and we will see yet another young author whose adventurous young hero lands her name on everybody's lips.

Maybe this author will be remembered.

What will the headlines say for this one?

Again, this is just a guess.

But Your Friendly Host honestly believes that the headlines will still be asking if she's the next J. K. Rowling. . . .

CHAPTER TWENTY-SIX

Unresolved Questions:
A Checklist

Feel free to mark up the following as you commence *Deathly Hallows*, with the understanding that Rowling is not obligated to resolve every last dangling plot point, not even in the long-completed final chapter that has been in her personal vault since before the completion of Book One.

Your Friendly Host provides several blank lines at the end of this chapter, for use jotting down questions that he may have overlooked. To avoid insane repetition, clauses involving variations of the phrase "assuming s/he survives" have been removed from all but a few of the questions below. Because of the nature of the story under discussion, it is to be assumed that the survival of any character remains in doubt, and therefore that any questions involving their future is rendered moot if they die deaths horrible or otherwise at any point in the final volume.

1. Will Harry succeed in killing Lord Voldemort?
2. Will he survive himself?
3. Will Ron and Hermione survive?
4. Assuming all three or any combination thereof survive, will they return to Hogwarts to complete their educations, once Voldemort is defeated?
5. If so, will the authorities force them to spend a last year attending classes, or just bow to the size of their accomplishment and provide them full credit for independent study?
6. Which characters among the good guys won't make it?
7. Which characters among the bad guys are going to get what they deserve?
8. Which of the following characters now listed as dead are, in fact, merely resting or pining for the fjords? The Potters?
9. Cedric Diggory?
10. Sirius Black?
11. Albus Dumbledore?
12. Where are the hiding places of the Horcruxes containing the fragments of Lord Voldemort's soul?
13. Are any of them at Hogwarts?
14. Will Harry, and Ron, and Hermione get to all of them in time?
15. Will they enter the final battle alone, or will Dumbledore's Army fight again?
16. What about the various members of the Order of the Phoenix?
17. Will anybody on Voldemort's side decide they want to help Dumbledore instead?
18. Conversely, will any member of Dumbledore's Army or the Order of the Phoenix do the unthinkable and turn traitor for the Dark Lord?
19. Will Neville Longbottom have another encounter with Bellatrix Lestrange?
20. Will he get to avenge his parents?
21. Will his Grandmother ever give him credit for anything?

22. Who gets to open a giant can of whup-butt on the deeply deserving Peter Pettigrew? Will it be Ron?

23. If not Ron, will Cruikshanks get to make a nice meal of Pettigrew's rat alter-ego, Scabbers?

24. Will Lucius Malfoy escape from Azkaban, and fight for his master in the final battle?

25. Will Draco Malfoy continue to show a conscience? Will he, in fact, turn out to be an unexpected ally?

26. If so, what will his mother Narcissa have to say about that?

27. Why has Dumbledore always been so adamant about trusting Severus Snape?

28. Was Severus Snape ever worth trusting?

29. If not, why has Dumbledore always been so deluded?

30. If so, what made Dumbledore so sure?

31. Who is R.A.B., the mysterious figure who beats Harry and Dumbledore to the Horcrux Voldemort stashed in the middle of that lake of corpses?

32. Is R.A.B. an ally or another dangerous enemy?

33. Is he or she somebody we've already met, or heard of? Or somebody new?

34. How did James Potter evolve from obnoxious if charming bully to the beloved husband of Lily?

35. If Snape and Harry remain enemies, will Harry have to fight his old teacher?

36. If Snape is revealed as an ally after all, will he and Harry ever make peace?

37. Assuming Harry wins, will his defeat of Voldemort be public knowledge?

38. What will the wizarding world think of him then?

39. Will he be commemorated on a Chocolate Frog card?

40. Will he still have enemies at the Ministry of Magic?

41. Will Rufus Scrimgeour still be eager to use Harry for political gain?

42. Will Dolores Umbridge still be working at the Ministry?

43. Will Harry get to confront Umbridge again?

44. Following the climax, will Hogwarts still be standing?

45. Will there still be a wizarding world, at all?

46. Who will be headmaster at Hogwarts?

47. Who will be the first Defense Against the Dark Arts Teacher to last more than one year?

48. Will Sybill Trelawney still have a job?

49. Will there be any closure during Harry's final visit with the Dursleys? Will Harry tell them off once and for all?

50. Is Dudley really going to be as miserable an adult as he is a child?

51. Does Petunia Dursley know any more about the magical world than she's let on?

52. Will Firenze the centaur be reunited with his people?

53. Will the centaurs join the fight? And on whose side?

54. Will the Dementors fight for Voldemort?

55. What part will the werewolves play?

56. Will Lupin get a chance to confront Fenrir Greyback, the werewolf that turned him?

57. Will Tonks and Lupin enjoy a happy future?

58. What is Dumbledore's amazing method of hiding people?

59. Who is he hiding?

60. Will Ron end up with Hermione?

61. Will Harry end up with Ginny?

62. Who on Earth will ever end up with Luna Lovegood?

63. What's going to happen to Grawp?

64. Will Rita Skeeter write any more exposes?

65. Will Hermione's parents, the Dentists, ever make another appearance?

66. Will Fleur's marriage to Bill Weasley go off without a hitch? Or, rather, with a hitch?

67. What wolfen characteristics will Bill pick up from the wounds inflicted by Greyback?

68. Will Percy Weasley ever realize that he's been a prat?

69. Will he apologize to his parents?

70. Will his siblings ever forgive him?

71. Will Fred and George continue their successful lives as captains of industry?

72. Will Hermione continue her social activism, with S.P.E.W. and other causes, after the battle with Voldemort is concluded?

73. If so, will she succeed in freeing the house-elves?

74. Will she make any headway turning around the wizarding world's oppressive treatment of other magical creatures?

75. If so, who'll do the dishes at Hogwarts?

76. Will Stan Shunpike ever be released from prison?

77. Will Mundungus ever be punished for looting the Black estate?

78. Will Gilderoy Lockhart recover his memory and take credit for everything?

79. Assuming Harry survives, what will he do with the riches he inherited from Sirius Black?

80. What will he do with Kreacher?

81. Will he ever return to the simple joys of Quidditch again?

82. Will he ever play professionally?

83. What will he choose for a career? Will he ever become the Auror he wants to be?

84. Or will he decide that he's had enough of fighting evil wizards and go into, let's say, teaching?

85. _____

_____

86. _____

_____

87. _____

_____

88. _____

_____

89. _____

_____

90. _____

_____

About the Author

Adam-Troy Castro sold his first article, a speculative work on the suicidal tendencies of whales, to *SPY* magazine. Now approaching his twentieth year as a published writer, he has a long list of credits that include articles, reviews, and short fiction for publications such as *Analog* and *The Magazine of Fantasy and Science Fiction*. His fiction has received multiple nominations for the Hugo, Nebula, and Stoker awards. His last book was the nonfiction *"My Ox is Broken!" Roadblocks, Detours, Fast Forwards, and Other Great Moments from TV's* The Amazing Race. His next books are the stand-alone horror novella *The Shallow End of the Pool* (coming soon from Creeping Hemlock Press) and the science fiction murder mystery *Emissaries from the Dead* (first of a series, coming in 2008 from HarperCollins). He is also working on a screenplay. Readers are invited to check out Adam-Troy's regular DVD reviews on www.Scifiweekly.com, and his book reviews in *Sci Fi* magazine. Artwork, rants, unpredictable other features, and news of other upcoming projects can be found at his Web site www.sff.net/people/adam-troy. Adam-Troy lives in Miami with his lovely wife Judi and a rotating assortment of cats that includes Uma Furman and Meow Farrow.